The
CREATIVE
WEDDING

JY

The CREATIVE WEDDING

Idea Book

BOLD SUGGESTIONS TO MAKE EVERY ASPECT OF YOUR WEDDING SPECIAL—FROM THE INVITATIONS TO THE HONEYMOON

JACQUELINE SMITH

BOB ADAMS, INC.
Holbrook, Massachusetts

Published by Bob Adams, Inc.
260 Center Street, Holbrook, MA 02343

ISBN: 1-55850-425-7

Printed in the United States of America.

J I H G F E D C B A

Library of Congress Cataloging-in-Publication Data
Smith, Jacqueline
    The creative wedding idea book : bold suggestions to make every aspect of your wedding special—from the invitations to the honeymoon / Jacqueline Smith.
        p. cm.
    Includes bibliographical references and index.
    ISBN 1-55850-425-7
    1. Wedding etiquette. 2. Weddings—Planning. I. Title.
    BJ2051.S57   1994
    395'.22—dc20   94-24754
                                                              CIP

This publication is designed to provide accurate and authoritative information with regard to the subject matter covered. It is sold with the understanding that the publisher is not engaged in rendering legal, accounting, or other professional advice. If legal advice or other expert assistance is required, the services of a competent professional person should be sought.
— From a *Declaration of Principles* jointly adopted by a Committee of the American Bar Association and a Committee of Publishers and Associations

This book is available at quantity discounts for bulk purchases.
For information, call 1-800-872-5627.

I dedicate this book to Frank, my loving and loved husband of thirty-one years, our wonderful children, Greg, Deb and Ray, and daughters-in-law, Sabrina and Amanda. Because of their reassurance, support and help, this book became a reality.

Special thanks to some old and wonderful friends. Melody Cassista for her assistance and encouragement and Sandy Byrne for her illustrative artwork.

Contents

Introduction   *xiii*

1. Changing Times—Changing Attitudes: It's Not Your Parents' Oldsmobile!   1

A Potpourri of Creative New Beginnings   2
Colorful and Fun Theme Weddings   7
Special Wedding Chapels to Accommodate Your Wedding   9
Personal Focus With Whispers of Who You Are   10
Making Your Wedding Your Own   11

2. Blast Off—Getting Ready to Be Creative: "I've Never Been Very Creative"   13

Gathering Creative Wedding Ideas   14
"By George, I Think We've Got It!"   19

3. Rainbows and Wedding Threads: Working Around Deciding Factors   21

A Perfect Size, Four to Twenty-four   21
A Closet Full of Dresses and No Wear to Go   22
How Did So Many Colors Get Into the Act?   23
Creating Your Wedding Picture   23
Disorderly Colors for Exciting Contrast   24
Patchwork Quilt Colors   26
Making or Helping to Make Your Own Wedding Dress   26
Alterations—Judging Competency   27
Wedding Apparel for Women in Waiting   27
Selecting Your Wedding Threads   28

4. "You Look Smashing!": "I Don't Want to Look Like a Mother"   33

What to Expect When You Start to Shop   34
Avoiding the Run Around   35
Complementing the Wedding Party   36
Designing the Perfect Dress for You   37

5. *Let Our Words Go Forth:*
   Invitations and Announcements with Personal Pizzazz   **41**
   Using Desktop Publishing to Design Your Invitation   41
   Exploring Other Creative Options   42
   Original Invitation Ideas   43
   Wedding Scrolls and Programs   45
   Preserving Your Invitation in Marble, Pewter, and Mirrors   48

6. *Take One—Lights, Camera, Action!:*
   Capturing Your Wedding Day History in Multiple Mediums   **51**
   Creative Professional Photography   51
   Creative Posing for Your Wedding Pictures   53
   Creative Wedding Photos to Consider   54
   A New Trend   56
   Creative Candid Shots   56
   Wedding Videos   57
   Montage Video   58
   Audiopictures®   59
   Stone Reproductions of Wedding Scenes   61

7. *Modest Income Designs:*
   Spinning Hay into Gold—La Creative Embellishment   **63**
   How to Look Expensive   64
   Working with What Is Available   65
   Using Your Mother's Wedding Dress   66
   Renting and Borrowing—It Can Be Done!   67
   "Something Borrowed . . ."   67
   Let Nature and Others Do the Decorating   68
   Make Your Own Music   68
   Small, Romantic, and Intimate—A Great Way Out for Some   69
   Call on a Posse of Elders to Help You   70
   File Those Receipts and Notes   70

8. *Going to the Chapel:*
   Church Weddings—Blending Old with New   **73**
   Creating a Personal Wedding Ceremony   73
   Music   74
   Examples of Prayers, Poems, Readings and Vows   76
   Things to Remember   88

9. "Let's Celebrate!":
Reception Recipes for Inclusion, Fun, and Excitement   **91**

"Do We Really Need a Head Table?"   92
Win/Win Seating for Your Guests   93
Raising the Roof with Music and Laughter   94
Wedding Cakes that Tell Who You Are   95
Remember Your Vegetarian and Non-Sugar-Eating Guests   96
For the Birds   96
The Scent of a Flower   98
Wedding Favors   99
"Insteadofs"   100

10. Memorable Toasts to Each Other:
Preserving the Moment Forever   **103**

11. Ethnic Themes:
Telling It Like It Is   **107**

African-American Ceremonies   108
Hispanic Ceremonies   112
Japanese Ceremonies   115
Additional Traits and Customs of Various Cultures   116

12. The Way We Are—Happy and Independent:
Creative Wedding Ideas for the Physically Challenged   **119**

"We Could Have Danced All Night!"   119
The Eyes Have It   112
A Sign of the Time   115
Some Additional Ideas   124

13. Away-from-Home Weddings:
"Don't Worry—Be Happy!"   **127**

Wedding License Requirements   129
Tying the Knot at Sea   130
Saying "I Do" at the Bottom, or Top, of the Grand Canyon   131
St. Kitts, West Indies   132
U. S. Virgin Islands Nuptials   133
Fiji—A "Blue Lagoon" Paradise for Your Ceremony   134

Antiqua–Caribbean Weddings   134
Moonlight (and Weddings) in Vermont   135
Rocky Mountain High Weddings   136
Bermuda Wedding Bells   137
A Castle Marriage in the City of Mozart   138
Spanish Bay Reef Weddings–Cayman Islands   139
Safari Weddings   140
Middlethorpe Hall, York, England   141
San Antonio Weddings   141
Apparel for Away Weddings   142
Wedding Travel Advisory   143
Distant Wedding Organizer and Departure Checklist   144
Selecting Your Travel Agent   147
The Reception/Celebration Party   149

14. **Turning Fantasy into Reality:**
     Weddings on the Move   **151**

"The Train, The Train!"   151
Weddings that "Take the Cake" and the Train   152
"Taking The A Train" in Scenic Vermont   155
"Up! Up! and Away in Our Beautiful Balloon!"   156

15. **Mixing and Matching:**
     Quick and Easy Ideas for Marriage Fun and Remembrance **159**

Prior to Your Big Day   159
The Day Itself   162
After the Wedding   165
Hand Me Down Customs and Ideas   167
Fanciful Ideas   170

16. **Turning a Sow's Ear into a Silk Purse:**
     Minimizing Problems and Addressing Crisis Situations **175**

An Ounce of Prevention . . .   177
Building Bridges with Uncooperative Family Members   178
Ten Salvaging Techniques   179

17. "Extra, Extra, Read All About It!": Creating Your Newspaper Byline — 183

Materials	183
Dress Descriptions	184
Necklines	185
Skirts and Waistlines	186
Sleeves	188
Hemlines	189
Trains	189
Details and Embellishments	189
Type of Lace	191
Veil Description	191
Types of Veiling	191
Types of Headpieces	192
Creating Your Byline	192

18. Creating "Magic Moments, Filled with Love": Keeping Romance Alive — 195

Taking the Time to Begin Anew	196
Renewing Your Marriage Vows	197
Creating a Lasting Marriage	198
Notable Quotations on Love and Marriage	200

Bibliography — 205

Index — 207

Introduction

So you're going to be married!   It is an important crossroad and a wonderful passage in life. There are many ways to prepare for marriage and there are two ways to give expression to preparation for monumental events such as this: "Da" or . . . "Ta Da!" Weddings plans should always be thought of as "TA DA!"

Personalizing all or part of your marriage ritual is one way to express "Ta Da!" and many couples are electing to do just this. They have received encouragement in this as there now exists more freedom for personal choice and expression, where once everything was dictated by church and custom. Adding your own thumb print to the ceremony and celebration is a way of gaining ownership of your marriage. Taking a more active part is both a desire and a reality for most couples today.

This book is written to help you with the "Ta Da!" of planning and personalizing your wedding celebration. It is a well full of creative ideas from which you can draw to spark your imagination and mold your own special day for lasting and loving memories. Remember, " It is imagination that both sets us apart and tightly binds our souls" (Author unknown). Congratulations and God Bless!

Jacqueline Smith

Chapter One

Changing Times—Changing Attitudes: It's Not Your Parents' Oldsmobile!

You have fallen in love and now plan to marry. There is no other feeling like it—two people committed to each other and to a lifetime together, generating new hopes and building new dreams. Your wedding day is the beginning of it all and should espouse this. Rightfully so, it should also reflect what is important to you both.

Today, many couples planning to be married are choosing to personalize and tailor their special day to their likes and needs, rather than simply following in the footsteps of their contemporaries or other family members. There is an increased focus on personal choice. Couples are turning to different wedding styles and sites for marriage, perhaps because these represent mediums or sacred environments that a particular couple can identify as their own. For your wedding, surround yourselves with people, things, and memories that have made you the special people that you are. The wedding will be more fun to put together, and a more memorable and meaningful day will be the outcome.

Departures from the norm of traditional wedding programs are now seen throughout the event, from the types of flowers and cakes used, to the creation of an entire wedding day based on a certain theme or place that holds the couple's interest. In addition to traditional religious weddings, couples may choose to be married on a mountain top, in the urban setting of an antique trolley car, or in a lush and fragrant garden, close to home or far away. A couple intuitively feel that here, on this special day of new beginnings, they can best identify and communicate their feelings of love. A kind of spirituality exists in these places for them. It is here that they are who they are.

Many people that witness these marriage ceremonies believe that a new wind is blowing. In finding their own sacred place, and selectively re-enacting old customs of marriage or creating new ones to be handed down, the modern couple is trying to insure that marriage once again will be long and lasting.

Using examples of how other creative couples are taking control of this rite of passage and personalizing their marriages, this chapter will encourage you to identify parts of the wedding scene that you may wish to make different and more special for your wedding day. Their stories will help sharpen your imagination and inspire you to acquire personal ownership of your marriage celebration, simply because it is your day to plan, to create, to love, and to enjoy.

A Potpourri of Creative New Beginnings

An older couple, both of whom had been widowed for some time, were getting married and wanted to include as many of their great grandchildren in the wedding as possible. Each of them had 10 children of their own so there were many children, grandchildren, and many, many great grandchildren to weave into the wedding ceremony. Being kind and sensitive people they knew that some loved ones' feelings might be hurt if just a few were asked to participate in the ceremony. They also found it impossible to make a decision on who would walk the bride down the aisle and who would act as flower girl and ring bearer.

The dilemma was resolved with a plan that quietly showed to everyone present in the church on the morning of their wedding day, what love is truly all about. The bride walked slowly, unescorted, down the aisle, carrying an empty flower basket. At every pew, she paused briefly, so that each grand child and great grandchild could place a flower in her basket. As she approached her handsome new groom, her basket was full of beautiful flowers from each family as a living symbol of the all-surrounding love they had created with their previous spouses, and the support given to them by their families for this new and loving union. This one small but otherwise personal touch set a special tone to the very traditional wedding celebration that followed.

By departing from the norm of the bride's being walked down the aisle by a particular person, they made their wedding ceremony more dramatic and meaningful for those involved and those attending the marriage. One of the guests said she felt an emotional tug at her heartstrings as the bride's basket was filled with flowers by all of the couple's youngest and smallest offspring: "It was a beautiful wedding to be at. It made me think about my husband and our children and the years that had passed and those that were yet to come. I think the scene made everyone present reflect on how special marriage and family truly is. It brought a joyful tear to my eyes."

Some couples are choosing to make a statement about their lives and roots through their wedding garb, and by making their ceremony more inclusive of children conceived or born before marriage. A wedding recently took place in my small community where the bride and groom were attired in period clothing of the American Revolutionary style and another groom met his bride at the wedding altar dressed in his Scottish kilt. The second marriage of another local couple involved their small child by having the flower girl push the child down the aisle in his baby carriage.

To honor their families and ancestors, many couples are having the wedding toasts done in several languages, to reflect their heritage. Most of us have colorful ancestries, and it's fun to see just how many languages can be incorporated into this exercise. The bridal party can be asked to do toasts in each of the different languages that reflect the bride's and groom's roots. Contacting a teacher involved with a language department at a nearby school or college will help you to find someone to do a proper translation if the language is no longer practiced within your family.

One bride and groom, whose parents were all divorced and remarried, asked each of them to think of something special to offer for the wedding ceremony or reception. They instructed each parent to put aside any feelings of bitterness or dislike that might have lingered and replace it with feelings of well-being and love for their children about to be married. A general truce was called for the wedding day. It worked well. The groom's parents stood before the reception party and, together, presented him and his new wife with a photo album of carefully selected pictures, showing how he came to be who he was. Next, with their new spouses, these four people kissed and hugged their child/step-child and new daughter-in-law.

The same bride has a deep interest in and love of quilts. Her mom consulted a professional quilt maker and with her help, designed a quilt that depicted various stages of her daughter's life while growing up at home. The place where the couple had met was the next to the last square. The last square was, of course, the wedding day scene. Her father was consulted and agreed to converse with the quilt designer on several squares that reflected how he viewed his daughter's important passages in life. The gift, a priceless heirloom for the young couple, was displayed at the door of the wedding reception hall. Needless to say, everyone was moved by this idea.

Perhaps one of the loveliest weddings I have witnessed was held high up on a mountain top. The bride, a teacher, was marrying a teacher and a ski instructor. Both she and her groom wanted to keep the ceremony simple but very memorable. The wedding and reception took place at the top of a ski mountain. The wedding party and the invited guests rode up to the site in chair lifts and the couple were married at a religious service on the side of the mountain. A ski lodge with beautiful views provided an ideal place for food, music, and dancing. An accordion player strolled about like a wandering minstrel, lending the air of a Swiss Alps affair to it all. Wildflowers were gathered in huge bouquets the day before and decorated the lodge. The bridal bouquet was even done with wildflowers. The couple had written their own marriage vows. Everything seemed to fit so well with the natural setting of the mountain side.

From the day that Bill asked Marsha to marry him, she had thought of all the things they would like to do for their wedding. He was a musician and she owned a travel agency. Both of them wanted to incorporate parts of their separate lives into their wedding theme. His idea was to have a dance along with the rehearsal dinner. He could easily get a group to play for it. One of her ideas was to use a lot of reggae music during their reception, as the Caribbean was a place they both loved, and many of their family and friends were also familiar with Caribbean travel. If they couldn't get married there, they would bring the Caribbean to New England! Another idea with which Marsha surprised Bill was having a red baseball cap on the head table for him and each of his groomsmen. He loved the game and they all belonged to a summer league. She was also going to have red satin shoe clips made and attach them to her shoes just before the garter toss was done. What a great surprise when he lifted the wedding dress to remove the garter. He loved the color red!

One couple who worked with the environment thought it would be nice if they provided their guests with seedlings to be planted in memory of their wedding day. Small seedlings were obtained from the state forestry department for very little money and these were set in paper cups the color of the wedding theme, with green bows attached. The groom was Irish so the green bows seemed perfect. They were put at each place setting as wedding favors. The couple estimates that over two hundred new trees were planted in their honor after their wedding day.

Another couple who were fond of horses had their faithful mounts waiting outside the church for them. To the delight and surprise of all their guests, they mounted their horses, the bride riding side-saddle, and trotted off a short distance to the reception site. They led the parade of cars carrying their guests. The horses themselves were decorated with long white taffeta blankets under their saddles, as in the days of kings and queens. In this way, the couple's wedding apparel was protected from soil. Arrangements had been made to have the horses pull an enclosed buggy that the couple could ride in, in case of inclement weather.

A New England couple whose lifestyle and education centered around the outdoor life held their wedding ceremony at a remote camp setting, located on a small lake in beautiful Vermont. The entire boy's camp was rented for the weekend. The cabins were used for their guests' sleeping accommodations.

Relatives and friends arrived on Friday night and the wedding was planned for the following morning. The ceremony took place outside, around the camp activities area, where the beautiful forest formed a small clearing. The celebration was family oriented, with lots of children present. The quiet and peaceful setting provided natural wonders as entertainment for all age groups. The wedding guests assembled at eleven o'clock in the morning at the secluded clearing where benches provided seating around a stone-enclosed circle, used previously for camp fires. The stone circle fire site was now filled with beautiful flowers and the couple's favorite classical music was played as guests took their seats.

The bride and groom in the meantime, had climbed into a canoe at another spot on the lake and were paddling around a point, to the sounds of the flute, to join their guests. The weather cooperated. The morning was sunny and warm and the lake was serene and calm. Several of their friends met them as they arrived at the shore of the camp site. The couple were then escorted by their friends and instrumental music up a short path to where the guests were assembled.

The couple's wedding attire was well chosen for their canoe "limo" and the ceremony's setting. The bride's apparel consisted of a pretty, soft white cotton dress with flowers in her hair. The groom wore dark pants and a white cotton shirt open at the neck. They each carried flowers for their parents, and after the families were recognized and warm embraces exchanged, the couple walked around the circle of flowers, family, and friends, to be seated at a special area among their assembly. Pieces of their favorite music were played throughout the ceremony by friends on woodwind instruments.

After the marriage ceremony a buffet reception was held in the upstairs loft of one of the camp buildings that overlooked the lake.

As night fell, a great fire was placed in the circle that had earlier held the wedding flowers. Once again, the now-married couple and their family and friends seated themselves around the warmth of the fire, for music and social entertainment. The bride's mother said the following about the wedding ceremony and reception: "The wedding fit their lifestyle. It was in tune with nature and what is important to them. It was a very beautiful and memorable day. The entire weekend was special in many ways."

The honeymoon that followed was also spectacular. The newly married couple set off several days later to climb the Appalachian Trail from start to finish, some two thousand miles that stretches from Georgia to Maine. Some of their wedding gifts were in line with their honeymoon plans and consisted of bed and breakfast certificates that would allow the couple to come off the trail from time to time and luxuriate for a spell along the way.

A very informal wedding was planned for late spring by one couple that were getting married for the second and third time. The bride had two small daughters from a previous marriage. Both wanted to have a ceremony that would include the children without a lot of stress and pressure.

She had grown up on a farm and chose a barn for their wedding service. "My dad used to have almost two hundred dairy cows. I always remember the barn as a warm, serene, comfortable, and special place. I had moved to a more suburban area after leaving home and always missed the animals on our farm. My girls of course loved farm creatures too." The couple had a friend who had a small farm and he agreed to have the ceremony in his barn and, per the request of the bride, "have some cows present!" The couple invited about 10 people to their small, intimate ceremony. However, as they approached the barn on the morning of the wedding, many other neighbors and friends, who had heard of this unusual wedding, had gathered to wish the couple well. To the surprise of the bride and groom, the inside of the barn had been decorated for the ceremony. Ten large, brown-eyed cows stood in their stanchions chewing their cud. Each had a colorful bow around its neck.

The couple were dressed in jeans and soft shirts to fit the setting and because an old-fashioned hay ride was planned to follow the ceremony. Guests had been told to dress for the occasion. The bride recalls that "some people even went out and bought new bib overalls to attend our wedding!" The bride carried wildflowers as did her two small daughters. The children were included in the wedding with a ring ceremony especially for them, following the couple's exchange of rings. The bride had bought two little gold knotted rings and had them blessed by the justice of the peace in front of the assembly. The children's mother and new father then placed the little rings on the girls' fingers, to make them feel a special part of this new family.

The ceremony went off without any hitches, except when the justice asked if there were any objections to the marriage. One of the great cows, who had stood quietly by until then, let out a long "Moo," as though it had rehearsed for this special moment. This sole objection was met with the eruption of spontaneous peals of laughter. A hay wagon picked up the entire crowd following the ceremony.

"The wagon was full of happy, laughing people. It was a lovely warm day with new life bursting out all over. The driver took us down a dirt road, through woods and meadows, and then down the main street of the rural town and on to the reception site, for food, music, and dancing. It was so much fun and such a great day. It was a wonderful new beginning for all of us."

ᕈ Colorful and Fun Theme Weddings

These are endless ideas to think about if you are considering a theme for your wedding day. Your clothing, food, and decorations can center around certain parts of the planet, or people, if you desire. Themes such as country and western, pirates, Star Trek, and a host of others may come to mind. The theme can command the entire focus of your wedding day, or just a small part, such as the wedding attire and cake.

A western couple who lived in Colorado and spent much of their lives on a ranch designed a wedding that incorporated some of the ranch life into the ceremony. They wanted "an old fashioned type of wedding day." The minister who performed the service reports that the wedding they designed was very much in character for them and seemed very appropriate.

A sheltered, grassy area was selected for the outdoor ceremony, within the U-shaped ranch building. The bride was dressed in a white satin wedding gown. She stood beside the minister and awaited her groom. He arrived on horseback along with his groomsmen and swooped down off his horse to stand next to his bride-to-be, dressed in western drover-style clothing.

The ceremony itself was not unusual, but at its conclusion the couple mounted their horses and galloped off some distance for their formal pictures, before returning to celebrate with their guests. The reception was held in the loft of a barn that they had wrapped in calico bows and other western-style decorations.

Historical themes are fun to do because everyone that is invited to the wedding becomes not only a guest, but also one of the main characters of the day. One couple had a beautiful wedding that stopped people in their tracks when they saw the bride and groom, their wedding party, and their guests entering the chapel. The bride, Diane Barr, is an award-winning custom designer of costumes and teacher of this trade. For her wedding, she and her future husband chose to be outfitted in beautiful, handmade, period dress of the 16th century..

Diane's gown was white and gold in a Renaissance style and Michael, her groom, dressed as King Henry the VIII. Their wedding party and 35 guests wore Elizabethan or Italian Renaissance costumes, which Diane had designed and created. To continue the theme, a minstrel played a 13th-century Shaum (oboe) as they all walked into the chapel. Diane designed and created beautiful invitations, wedding programs, and a wedding certificate with the help of a local desktop publisher. Each was done in Gothic print, on parchment paper, and illuminated with gold ink and a gold filigree border. A reception "feast," eaten with fingers only, and a jousting tournament added to the authenticity of their historical theme wedding day.

> Because everyone was dressed like court members of this period, they became an interwoven part of our wedding celebration. Many guests said that they felt very special, like royalty or celebrities. Our guests were photographed almost as much as we were. Getting married in period costume is romantic, beautiful, and very creative.

Since her wedding, Diane has become a wedding consultant, specializing in costumed weddings. Along with her friend, Yvonne Sutherland, who is an event coordinator, they research, design, and plan weddings with period themes. "We can do any theme from Medieval to Victorian and beyond. Our costumes are dramatic, authentic looking, and well made." Both rental and custom design options are available and prices range from about $50-$300 for rental outfits and $500 and up for custom-designed wedding attire for bride, groom, wedding party, and guests. Lead time for obtaining a period design wedding costume is two to three months. "All that is really needed is an idea of what you want and true body measurements."

More information about this wedding option can be acquired by writing or calling: Rose Dzynes, 1196 Sunglow Drive, Oceanside, California 92056, 1-619-941-3582 or 1-800-899-ROSE, or Alexis Event Coordinators, 537

Newport Center Drive, #209, Newport Beach, California 92660, 1-714-760-4476.

❧ Special Wedding Chapels to Accommodate Your Wedding

Over the past several years, small wedding chapels have grown up to meet the changing needs of a multicultural society. These wedding chapels, formerly found only in a select area of the country, are now coming into their own in many states. Cross-cultural couples and couples of mixed religions are but two groups to which the idea of being married in a small wedding chapel appeals. Because these non-denominational chapels are more open and accepting of couples of mixed races, cultures, and religions, the road from engagement to marriage has been made easier.

Couples with very focused interests are also using wedding chapels for their marriage services. Donna Wilson and Rhoda Barzak, owners of White Rose Weddings, located in Ormond Beach, Florida, are two wedding consultants and "creators of total wedding magic." In addition to helping couples design weddings to meet their individual cultural and lifestyle needs, they have recently built a new wedding chapel to accommodate many different types of wedding parties.

> Because we are so close to Daytona Beach and the motorcycle culture that descends on the area each spring, we have done several weddings with the theme of "leather and lace." These professional couples were very much attuned to motorcycles as hobbies and for their special day, they used white leather outfits for their ceremony. They arrived at the wedding chapel on motorcycles, along with their attendants and several of their guests. At one particular ceremony, the bride even wore a leather headpiece with a short lace veil attached to it. It can be very exciting to watch the bride and groom ride into the chapel grounds with a small contingency of their friends giving them a motorcycle escort. Following the ceremony, they all rode off to a reception party together, followed by those with bikes first and then those with more conventional modes of transportation.

If you would like to consider a "Leather and Lace" wedding, more information is available by calling 1-904-673-5535.

◆ Personal Focus With Whispers of Who You Are

The following ideas are just a few to get you started thinking about the unlimited possibilities for your own wedding. Many more are found throughout this book, but the most important thing is to choose the ones that are right for you.

Create a wedding day diary. Place a block of colored paper and pen on each table of the reception with a warm welcome note on the first page. Instruct your guests to jot down a thought, note, or wish for the wedded couple, throughout the wedding reception. When collected and placed together at the end of the day, these writings will represent a vivid historical account of your special day, through the eyes of family and friends.

Commission an artist to sketch various scenes from the ceremony and reception. Simple pen and ink renditions of special moments will evoke powerful memories in years to come. Watching the artist at work also provides entertainment for your guests. (Perhaps you have friends that can sketch well. Ask them to do this as a wedding gift to you.)

If small children, ages three or under, are going to participate in the ceremony as flower girl or ring bearer, help them with the difficult task of walking down the aisle by incorporating their doll carriage or little cart. The decorated doll carriage can have wedding dolls, baby dolls, and so on in it, and a basket of flowers can be hung on the front. The little boy's cart can carry lots of flowers and some of his favorite toys or stuffed animals, with the ring pillow as a centerpiece. This type of scene touches people's hearts and reinforces what love and marriage is all about: home and family. If you have a lot of nieces and nephews that would like to be in your wedding but you can choose only one, ask the rest of them to dress as their favorite "Sesame Street" character to celebrate your wedding!

Have one of your attendants collect a thumb print and the name of their favorite animal from each of your guests on special note cards during the reception. Have an artist do a "thumb print picture" of your guests' favorite animals, using the thumb prints for their faces. You can use these personal cards to send out after the reception as thank you notes for wedding gifts. Sketch artists can usually be found at state or craft fairs and generally charge about one dollar per picture. The picture can be cropped to fit a mini picture frame. Your guests will all want to keep this personal keepsake of your wedding after it is received.

The bride and groom can also use this idea to have a personal sketch done of a pair of their thumb prints, decorated in wedding attire, and frame it for a wedding keepsake for their home. See the samples in Figure 1.1. (Call your local hospital and ask them to save some of the ink cards they use to take baby foot prints. These cards will allow you to collect your thumb prints and those of your guests without leaving any inky thumbs!)

Figure 1.1
Sample thumb print sketches

✒ *Making Your Wedding Your Own*

Now it is your turn to plan and design a unique and special day for your marriage and the celebration of this wonderful passage in life. As you set out to do this, do not be afraid to be different and to use your own imagination. Let some or all of your wedding plans represent your true spirits and the special qualities you bring to one another. Feel free to focus on that medium of expression that readily suits both of you, and build your wedding day around it.

If color is your anchor to happiness and you strongly identify with it, let color lead the way. Use bold, striking colors in every imaginable way in all parts of your wedding plans. If motion is the medium that frees you and allows a deeper, intimate communication of your spirit with that of your new mate, find a way to incorporate this into your wedding day. Get married on a ship or aloft in a hot air balloon. If sound is the well from which you draw daily strength and rebirth, weave the sounds that peak your senses into your wedding scene.

Let your imaginations run wild and free at the onset of your planning stage. Pick and choose which ideas will work best and be the most meaningful for you as individuals and together as a couple. Using creative interpretation, you can incorporate what is special about each of you to truly personalize this most important day in your lives. In doing so, your wedding day will take on a much deeper tone and feeling than if you simply follow a plan that belongs to someone else. Like creatively decorating your own home, your entire marriage ceremony and wedding celebration will feel comfortable and make sense to you. The process of getting to that special day can be fully appreciated by both you and your family and friends who witness your marriage or take an active part in it. Perhaps even more importantly, by creating your own personal blueprint, you will be preparing for the marriage as well as preparing for the wedding day.

Chapter Two

Blast Off—Getting Ready to Be Creative

"I've Never Been Very Creative"

If you want creative and original ideas for your wedding celebration but seem to have a hard time conceptualizing or being creative read on. Unlike people such as Mozart or Disney who had imaginations that were constantly in overdrive and allowed them to create wonderful sounds and ideas, many of us need stimulation to get our imaginations into gear which will then allow us to be creative too.

The first step in being creative is to visualize. Most of us need help in this area to some extent. Stimulating your senses of sight, smell, sound, taste and touch is one way to help you visualize concepts and to awaken the creative urges that lie deep within. Creative juices do flow within each of us. They just need to be allowed to flow and to bubble up to the surface of our brain. Stimulating your five senses will cause this to happen.

An easy and fun way to do this is to spend a day or two visiting places in your area that do just that. This simple exercise will make both of you more aware of different things that can be used to create personal touches for your wedding plans. It will help you see how things that are readily available can be molded to fit your wedding day needs. When you next go out to shop and contract for your wedding services, you will have a better vision of what you want and what is needed to bring the wedding day of your dreams into clear focus.

Each of you should bring a small notebook along to jot down ideas as things start to bubble up and pop into your head. After you get a book full of colorful and exciting ideas for your wedding design, pick a special place and go out to lunch together to discuss and review which ideas and thoughts will work the best for the two of you. Planning your special day should always be fun and exciting and each part of it should be planned out together. This starts your wedding plans off on an easy note. Some of the places that you might want to explore to stimulate your imagination and senses and to help you be creative with your wedding plans are

> *A garden shop (smell, sight, touch)*
> *A fabric store (sight, touch)*
> *A crafts store (sight, touch)*
> *A hardware store (sight, touch)*
> *A fruit market (smell, sight, taste)*
> *A bake shop (smell, taste, sight)*
> *A music store (sound)*
> *A bookstore or library (sound)*
> *A candy store (sight, smell, taste)*

~ Gathering Creative Wedding Ideas

Stimulating your five senses is like putting a sparkplug to your imagination. This will put you, whoever you are, into a very creative mode, and ideas to personalize your wedding will quickly start to pile up. Let's meander through these places to see how the process works, using just a few examples in each area.

A Garden Shop

A visit to your local garden shop is a great place to start to get ideas for wedding receptions that are planned for outdoors or indoors. Among other things, you can get easy ideas for creating some of your own floral decorations. Here are just a few ideas that could be used for your party and used again for your home later on:

Hanging Poles and Hanging Plants. If you want to hold your reception at your home or that of a parent during the spring and summer months, this is a great way to dress up the yard and give it a very festive flavor. Wrought iron poles are available that screw into decks or easily push into the ground. They come in various heights and are designed with hooks much like a coat rack, so that each pole can accept several hanging pots of flowers.

You can either buy potted flowering plants to hang on the poles or grow your own. Thousands of plastic pots that contained annual plants are thrown out each year at the end of the summer season. If you want to secure your pots for free and recycle some plastic in the process, ask your family, friends, co-workers, and neighbors to save their discarded pots to be used again for flowers to decorate your wedding site or yard. Buy new potting soil and flower seeds to suit your fancy. Plant your seeds, working within the time frame necessary to give you beautiful blooms just in time for your wedding day. The poles can be spread indiscriminately around the yard or placed side by side in a semi-circle to form a special place where you can stand to speak your vows. After the party is over, you will have the poles to use again to beautify your home each summer season as a wonderful reminder of your wedding day. The plastic pots can be returned to their owners, full of your wedding flowers as a special thank you for their help.

Baskets of Various Sizes and Shapes. Baskets make great containers for floral arrangements, wherever and whenever your wedding is going to take place. Some of them, such as plain old apple baskets, are readily available and very inexpensive (about four dollars each). They are easy to fill and can be dressed up to look pretty for wedding scenes.

You can fill baskets with flowers in many ways. A collection of flowering plants can be set inside each basket. Usually a group of three pots of flowers will make a large apple basket look full. The bottom can be filled with old newspaper to allow the pots to sit toward the top of the basket. The spaces in between each pot can be filled in with greens cut from a hedge or a tree. Add a big bow to each basket to bring out your wedding colors. Simply tie it to the side of the basket or wire it to a long stick and push it down into one of the plants. Pumpkins and chrysanthemums can be set into the baskets for fall wedding scenes. Depending on the types of potted flowers you use, you can set large floral baskets out to decorate your wedding scene for less than $20 each.

Large apple baskets also work well using a mixture of home-grown flowers or wild flowers. Perhaps you have someone that always has beautiful flower gardens and would be willing to provide you with flowers for your wedding day decorations. Perhaps you have the time and space to grow your own arrangements. After the celebration, the handy baskets can be reused for a string of other creative projects or can be taken home by any of your guests who wish to pick apples in the fall.

Colorful Bulbs. The bigger garden shops will have a supply of beautiful bulbs that will bloom in every imaginable color at various times of the year. They are easy to grow, even for those who do not have a green thumb.

Simply place them in fresh soil and water them regularly. This is an inexpensive way to add your own colorful flowers to any wedding plan. Watching them grow is fun and exciting, and a refreshing way to count down to your wedding day. Pots of colorful flowers also make great gifts for the wedding party to take home after the wedding.

Bird Baths and Japanese Stepping Stones. These garden accents may be just what is needed to spruce up the place you have in mind for your reception party. The bird bath could be purchased and kept for later use, especially if you love to watch the wonders of nature. They now come in all sorts of shapes, designs, and colors. There are even heart-shaped bird baths! You may want to use one as a focal point in your reception scheme or for the place where you will exchange your marriage vows. They can be used to beautify an outdoor or indoor site.

A bird bath can also be used as a wishing well where your guests can cast coins into the water along with good luck wishes for your marriage. If you plan to use your bird bath this way, set a small colorful pad of paper, a pen, and some scotch tape nearby so your guests can write down their wedding wish for you and attach it to the bird bath after they cast their coin into it. Everyone likes to make wishes!

Japanese stepping stones depict the four seasons with a picture and Japanese character for each season, written on the face of the stone. They are round in shape, about the size of a pie pan, and are light-weight but very sturdy. You might want to set these on the path that you will walk down toward the place of the ceremony. Stepping on the different seasons can be viewed as symbolic of the circle of time that you will live as a married couple. The stones can be placed in your flower garden or in a path to the door of your home following your wedding celebration, as a cognitive reminder of your special day.

Herbs. There are over one hundred different types of herbs, many of them used in parts of the wedding scenes of long ago. Their scents and meanings can give poetic beauty to your wedding decorations and floral arrangements (see chapter fifteen). The ones you select for use in your ceremony can later be used as potted plants for your home, for wedding day remembrances and for "cooking with love" throughout the year.

Flowering Trees. You can buy a flowering tree to beautify the wedding scene or to stand beside for your wedding vows. It can be placed in a decorated apple basket for the ceremony, inside or outside, and later planted in the yard of your home or that of your parents. As the years pass, it will grow into a majestic and beautiful reminder of your marriage.

A Fabric Shop

If you have never used a sewing machine or have little knowledge of sewing, a visit to a fabric shop will open your eyes to color, style, and types of fabrics that you can select for your wedding scheme. Some examples:

Big Color Swatches. Bridal shops typically have quite small sample swatches of materials in different colors and types, to use for ordering wedding apparel. Small swatches of colored or printed material always appear less vivid and bright, which can be confusing. Before you go to the bridal shop to select your attendants' dresses, go into a fabric shop and look at different colors and types of material by unwrapping the bolts and placing large pieces of material next to each other. This will help you to visualize better how different colors and types of material complement each other, so you can create the best look for your wedding party.

Accessory Items. A must-see in any fabric shop is the notions department. Here you can get ideas for making (or having made) many different types of hair decorations. Sequins, lace trim, and lots of other small detail items can be the ingredients needed to give an imaginative touch to your accessory items, or if you want to change the look of a certain piece of apparel.

A Crafts Store

This is a place where any imagination can be lit up in lights. A well-supplied crafts store can give you many ideas to accent different parts of your wedding. You will find many different and inexpensive how-to books on crafts that will lead you step-by-step through the different processes, if you have not exercised your craft skills before.

Silk Flowers. If you think that you want to make some or all of your floral arrangements, you will find all the items needed to do the job here. It is easy, fun, and relaxing to make your own flowers for your wedding and this can be done many months ahead of time. Simple arm held bouquets of flowers can easily be put together. Wander through the silk flower section of a crafts store and pick them as you would from a flower garden. Select different kinds and sizes of flowers, using the smaller ones like forget-me-nots and dried baby's breath as "fillers" to make your bouquets look full. You can buy green paper tape, called florist tape, to wind around each stem, to make them look real or to bind all the stems together into one. Adding bows and long ribbon streamers to your bouquets will give them a professional look and finish off your project.

Wedding Favors. You can find all types of little items that can be wrapped up in different squares or rounds of material or paper to use as small tokens of love and appreciation. Tiny heart shaped, pretty-smelling pieces of soap, little straw hats, or containers for candy are some of the items you may find here. This is another part of the wedding that can be done ahead of time and a wonderful and fun exercise that you can do together as a couple.

Attendants' Gifts. If you want to give your attendants gifts with meaning, make them yourself using your own ideas and the tools and supplies you will find in a crafts store. It is a fun and exciting way to get things ready for your wedding day and it will give you a feeling of accomplishment as you proceed with your other wedding plans.

A Hardware Store

An artist friend of mind once said that she "went crazy looking at all the little things that could be used to be creative!" as she accompanied her husband into a hardware store one day. She bought a handful of small wooden knobs of various sizes and created a chess set and a small nativity scene, by hand painting faces of the various characters on the shaft of each knob. The top of the knobs made a natural hat for the face. Using this idea, a "wedding" chess set could be created making the groom the king, the bride the queen, and so on. It would make a special thank-you gift for your best man, maid of honor, or for your parents if any of these people enjoy chess. Try looking at the contents of a hardware store through the eyes of an artist and you may come away with other unusual and creative ideas that can be used for wedding remembrances.

A Fruit Market

Fruit will add color and a different taste to your wedding reception. Platters of fruit can be used as centerpieces for your tables instead of or in combination with flowers. Special pieces of fruit can be decorated in tulle and ribbons and used as a wedding favor such as the delicious kiwi. Colorful fruit can have a special place at your party, just as it did in the days of kings and queens.

A Bake Shop

Here is where you can spark up your sense of smell, taste, and sight to design the wedding cake of your dreams. Take an idea from here and another from there and go to the person who will bake your wedding cake with a specific type of personal cake design in mind.

Perhaps you would like to have a pastry cart at your celebration party, filled with different types of delicious smelling pastries, so your guests can individually select a small gourmet dessert following the meal. Pieces of the wedding cake can then be wrapped and given out as wedding favors for your guests to take home as a taste of your wedding day.

A Music Store

The melody and lyrics of the music that you use for your ceremony and reception will also set a particular tone to your wedding day. Perusing the vast selections available to you will help you remember oldies and discover new sounds and words that feel just right for your wedding scene.

A Bookstore

If you want to create your own vows, your own words for your exchange of rings, or to interject your own personal reflections throughout your marriage ceremony, perusing prose and poetry will start you in the right direction. This will help you find the right words to articulate your feelings about love and marriage to each other as you stand to solemnize your marriage. An antique book store may be another source for finding just the right words that will make the ceremony yours.

A Candy Store

A special sweet from a special place can be given as wedding favors to tickle the fancy of your invited guests. You can select a mixture of different types of candy that would work well as favors. Cover each piece in foil and wrap it in a piece of tulle with a ribbon and small card with your names and wedding date, or a tiny thank-you note. Whenever you enter a candy store or smell the wonderful odors coming from one in the future, pictures of your wedding day will drift before you and bring back memories of this special time.

ᴖ "By George, I Think We've Got It!"

Being creative is not difficult when you stimulate your imagination. Creative ideas can be woven into each part of your ceremony and reception party, if you get your imaginations into gear, allow yourself enough time to complete the various projects that you will want to do, and work as a team to accomplish this end. Adding your personal touches makes the day belong to you. Using creative ideas can make the wedding more joyful and exciting for everyone involved.

Chapter Three

Rainbows and Wedding Threads

Working Around Deciding Factors

Setting out to select the styles and colors of your wedding apparel is exciting and fun. Most couples have an idea in mind for the colors they would like to use before they begin to shop. Taking a few minutes to think about a few "deciding factors" that you will have to work with or work around will make the job easier. Some of the important things to consider when selecting the color and styles of your attendants apparel are:

1. *Body frames and sizes*
2. *Wearability*
3. *Your ceremony setting*
4. *Your reception setting*

Using your favorite colors should come first, but you also need to give consideration to these other factors when making your selections. If you can fit them all together in a complementary mode you will maintain better harmony for your entire wedding scene and keep your attendants as supportive friends.

A Perfect Size, Four to Twenty-four

Bridesmaids will usually be several sizes apart and it can be difficult finding garments that will look good on their different body frames. Concentrate on the cut of the dress first. Will it look good on all of the attendants? A simple, basic cut generally looks good on everyone. Does it comes in the colors that you want to use for your wedding? If not, you can work around this by doing one or more of the following:

1. Have the maid of honor's dress made of your favorite color and buy the other dresses in an available, contrasting color.

2. Use your favorite color to accessorize your wedding and to bring out your color focus. Hair combs, hats, gloves, shoes, ribbons, and flowers can act as vivid accents. In many art forms, it is the accents that make the statement memorable.

3. Have all your dresses made. Some brides simply buy a pattern and material for each bridesmaid's dress and send it off to them to be made by a seamstress close to where they live. The main thing here is to be certain that there is a qualified seamstress doing the construction in each case. The cost of making dresses should coincide with preconstructed garments of a similar design. A good seamstress can create a dress in a relatively short period of time.

Be sure to specify the finished length of the dress so they will all look similar in length for your wedding photos. This is easily done by having them all hemmed eight inches off the floor in stocking feet. This measurement will create a tea-length hemline. Using the same size heel will make the hem lines even for your pictures. For a shorter hemline, simply increase the number of inches off the floor the hem should be in stocking feet.

4. Find a dress that is available in both solid and print materials. This will give more versatility for outfitting different body frames and let you mix and match according to what looks best on each person. Printed dresses let you draw out one of several colors that can be used for matching solid colored dresses. Some companies are now producing a few dress styles for bridesmaids that come in both solid and print material for this reason.

ᴥ A Closet Full of Dresses and No Wear to Go

An important consideration for your bridesmaids, especially if they have already been in several weddings, is for them to be able to wear their dresses again. Special-occasion dresses for weddings are different from other clothing, but with a little thought on your part in the selection process, your bridesmaids can wear their dresses again to other functions.

The type of material you select for your bridesmaids' dresses will largely determine their wearability. Cotton blends and print dresses can be dressed up for a wedding and dressed down for casual wear. Satin and taffeta dresses in jewel tone colors can always be used again at holiday time. Satin and taffeta dresses in solid pastel tones are difficult to use again for any event. If you have your heart set on a satin or taffeta, pastel bridesmaid dress for your wedding, think about how your friends will react to this idea first. If they seem hesitant, offer to pay for some of the dress to sweeten your color selection just a little and keep your friendship on a happy note.

✣ How Did So Many Colors Get into the Act?

If your ceremony and reception setting are in a place that is done in neutral tones, any color combination that you select for your attendants' apparel will fit in well. If bright or bold colors have been used to decorate these areas, you need to give some thought to selecting wedding colors that not only harmonize among themselves, but also with the area in which they will be used. This will give a more harmonious look to everything overall.

As the wedding of one couple drew near, the bride asked the person in charge of the reception site about using pink table cloths to match her pink bridesmaids' dresses. Neither she nor her mother realized, until it was pointed out to them a few weeks before the wedding, that the chair coverings at the reception setting were orange and yellow. "We were so busy thinking about other things the day that we contracted for the site that we just didn't notice this little detail."

If you still want to use your favorite colors in a setting that seems opposed to them, think about what you can do to make them fit in. Can off-white chair covers be rented to convert the seating to a neutral color? If the chairs can't be changed in some way, could the table cloths be changed to a neutral color to tone things down? Could you use all ivory or white floral arrangements to soften the scene and make it more acceptable to your dress colors? Would using a softer tone of your favorite color fit in better? By making some simple adjustments, rooms or furniture of opposing tones can be made to harmonize better and blend in with your wedding colors.

✣ Creating Your Wedding Picture

Questions about colors and styles and how they fit together with each other are always a concern to couples. Generally speaking, there is no one set of rules to go by any more. Dark colors are now used in the summer as much as light colors. Light colors are sometimes used late into the fall and even during the winter months. Once certain styles of tuxedos were only worn at certain times of the day or evening. Now, all styles of tuxedos are acceptable at weddings regardless of the time of the ceremony. Some brides are now having each bridesmaid wear a different dress, instead of dressing them all in identical garb. Sometimes the bride may indicate a preference in color but allow each bridesmaid the freedom to exercise her own personal taste in style so she can wear the dress again to many functions.

You have probably attended or heard about several weddings where the bridal party and all the immediate family members were dressed in the same color. I once attended one in which everyone was dressed in the bride's favorite color, peach. Even the female relatives attending the wedding dressed in peach dresses because the bride loved this color! In another wedding ceremony, everyone except the great grandmothers were dressed in blue. The two grand matriarchs were attired in yellow. Yet another wedding scene presented the entire wedding party dressed in white while the bride wore a wedding dress of soft pink tones.

A trend that has become popular during the last several years is to use cotton print dresses for the bridesmaids' attire. Cotton is a comfortable fabric to wear because it is a natural fiber that allows the body to breathe. A print dress can be dressed up for the wedding with a fluffy petticoat and haircomb of matching fabric. When the petticoat and haircomb are removed, the dress can be put to everyday use more easily than the satin and taffeta materials traditionally used for bridesmaids apparel. Cotton print dresses with large, bold-colored flowers can even be used to complement very formal satin and silk wedding dresses.

If a combination looks good to you and seems to go together don't hesitate to use it just because it hasn't been done before. Couples should enjoy the freedom of designing and decorating their wedding in much the same way they will decorate the rooms of their home. Today it's a matter of personal choice more than anything else.

❧ Disorderly Colors for Exciting Contrast

I am frequently asked by brides who are starting to piece together the colors for their wedding if they go together all right. Perhaps because there are also many different shades and tones of color available to choose from, this exercise can sometimes seem confusing. As in music, where two or more harmonious sounds are blended together, there are many ways to strike a harmony using various color combinations. There are a few basic and easy rules that should be followed to help you use your favorite color and select others that will harmonize well with it.

All color is derived from three colors, red, blue, and yellow. Think of a triangle within a wheel with one of these colors at each of the three points. All the various shades and tones of color are derived from these three colors and fill the spaces on the wheel as you proceed from one of the major color points to the next. A color wheel will show how different color combinations can be used successfully to achieve an overall harmonious effect.

You can fill in the spaces on the color wheel with many of the in-between colors and then play with the different color combinations. This will help and encourage you to be inventive and original when choosing your color combinations or color accents for your wedding celebration. Go to your nearest paint store and select several cards with all the "filler" colors for those in between the basic colors of red, yellow, and blue. Tape these colors to your wheel in their appropriate places and use this tool to help you envision color combinations for your wedding. Looking at where colors are positioned on the wheel, there are several standard ways of achieving color harmony:

Monochord Harmony—using different shades of the same color
Analogous Harmony—using neighboring colors
True Harmony—using two colors directly across from one another
Split Harmony—using three harmonious colors. Select two true colors, or two that are directly opposite each other on the color wheel, and then deviate to the right and left sides of one of the two colors to select two more colors, for a total of three colors that will blend well together.
Triadic Harmony—an easy way to use multiple colors in harmony is to simply select three colors that are equal spaces apart on the color wheel.

Sometimes colors that don't seem to match can be put together effectively by using a lighter shade or deeper tone. A good example would be red and orange, which used to be thought of as opposing colors that fought each other. They create an analogous harmony because they are neighboring colors. Using them together in different shades and tones has created a very warm look in fashion wear today.

❧ Patchwork Quilt Colors

Different prints and designs can also be used well together. You need only to think of a patchwork quilt to imagine seemingly opposing prints that have been fitted together to make an appealing and beautiful overall design. A great country wedding theme could be achieved by using a patchwork print material in different harmonious colors. A single color that harmonizes with the print could be used for the flowers and other wedding accents. Another idea might be to use a patchwork print dress for the maid of honor and pick up a different solid color in the print for each of the bridesmaids' dresses.

Some couples are now starting to think of mixing and matching tuxedos and sports coats at wedding scenes. At two recent formal weddings, the groom dressed in a navy tuxedo while his groomsmen wore regular navy sports jackets with off-white pants. At yet another, the groom's attendants wore their own navy sports jackets, and all of them bought new Nantucket red sports pants. Each had a different tie that matched his outfit, a gift from the bride and groom.

❧ Making or Helping to Make Your Own Wedding Dress

If you have ample time and are good at sewing, you may wish to create your own wedding dress. Some brides that cannot sew may decide to have their dress made because they cannot find exactly what they want or are difficult to fit. If you find a dress that you like but want to alter several things on it, it may be easier for everyone involved to simply start from scratch. A good seamstress will be able to advise you which path is easiest.

A good compromise between making and buying a wedding dress is to have the shell made by an experienced seamstress, and for you to hand sew the beading or the lace that you want to add to the dress. Once the beads and sequins have been added to the lace, the lace can then be hand sewn to the different parts of the dress, by you alone or in conjunction with the help of your seamstress. One bride that I worked with added beading and sequins to the hem and train of her dress. This gave the dress a little more sparkle, which was what she was looking for, and made her feel involved with the creation of her wedding dress. It also made an average wedding dress look a touch more expensive and special.

Alterations—Judging Competency

Before you hire someone to do original construction or entrust him or her to alter a garment to fit, you should be sure that he or she is a professional at this work. Almost anyone can sew with a little basic knowledge. Having a dress made or altered properly, however, requires fine-tuned sewing skills and sometimes more than just a sewing machine. Seams that are ripped out should always be finished off with a serger that wraps the seam edge in thread to prevent fraying. Just as you look at the samples of the work of others, like the florist, photographer, and musicians, it is important to ask to see some of the work of the seamstress who will be handling your apparel.

Focus on such things as outside and inside seams. Check to see that the outside seams are straight and that "raw edges" of inside seams are finished off with a serger stitch. (A serger machine is used to cast a continuous thread over the seam edge to prevent fraying.) Examine how one seam fits into another. Look to see how well a sleeve has been set into a garment. If there are gathers on the garment, are they set in with an even effect overall? If there is an obvious pattern in the material, does the pattern match up at the seam lines, so that the pattern flows through the garment without interruption?

To prevent problems down the road, be sure to find out if the seamstress can alter an apparel pattern if need be. A skilled person can do all of these things with relative ease. This helps to insure that the results of an altered or a garment made to order, will fit properly and look well-made.

Wedding Apparel for Women in Waiting

It is not an infrequent thing today that one of the bridesmaids will be pregnant. Finding a dress to match the others can be an impossible task. Also, the bride may find herself in this condition and not be able to find a wedding dress to complement her growing figure. At this point in time, the apparel industry has failed to address this issue.

There are two obvious things that can be done. One is to buy a pattern and have a dress made, and the other is to alter an already-constructed dress to fit the pregnant figure. Altering a dress is usually less time-consuming and less expensive. Any dress can be disconnected at the waistline and reattached to the bodice higher up under the bustline. This gives the dress a graceful "empire," or raised-waistline, look and also accommodates the growing abdomen for comfort.

If the dress is going to be ordered and there is a question of what size to order, it is usually safe to order it one or two sizes bigger than your regular size. In addition to raising the waistline, the side seam of the bodice can then be taken in or let out to fit the bustline properly.

If you have a dress but the bodice is too small, a "gusset," or extra piece of material, can be set into each side seam of the bodice. Depending on the original length of the dress and the height of the person it is being altered for, a ruffle may or may not have to be added to the hemline to achieve the desired length. Generally, if you start with a floor length dress, there is ample length available to allow for turning the dress into an empire style without having to add on to the hem for length.

❧ Selecting Your Wedding Threads

Shopping for wedding apparel is something like sailing into uncharted waters! It is a different type of buying experience because it is a specialty type of business with time frames and multiple people involved in the process. Knowing the right questions to ask can make the sail smoother, more trouble free, and generally insure your survival. Asking these simple questions before you order your apparel can save you time, money, and frustration as you venture into the sea of matrimony.

What type of a size chart is this dress cut to? All the manufacturers use different size charts to cut their garments and some use a more generous cut than others. A more generously cut garment is indicative of quality and can eliminate costly alterations, because it generally fits better to begin with. Using size 10 as an example, a good cut for a size 10 is bust 36" and waist 28". All the other sizes should be relative to this by about one-and-one-half inches, up and down the size chart.

What color material does this bridal dress come in? Most companies now cut all their wedding dresses in white and ivory. Some are also cut in soft pastels because not everyone looks good in white. If you are looking for a wedding dress in a color other than white, you will want to know this up front before you fall in love with a dress that you cannot get in your color.

What type of material is this dress made of and does the price reflect the quality of construction? Satin is the most frequently used material to construct wedding dresses. Other types of material are taffeta, shantung, brocade, cotton, silk, and various blends. Also, there are different weights to each material. Generally the heavier the weight of the material, the more expensive it is. The type and quality of the material and the construction and workmanship, should be tied directly to the price of the dress.

What type of lace is used as embellishment? There are several types of lace. Generally, the lighter the lace, the less expensive it is. Alençon lace is one of the most expensive. The type of lace and the amount used as embellishment will also be reflected in the price.

How long will it take to get the dress once I place my order? Most wedding dresses can be produced in a 10-week time frame. A few may take as long as 16 weeks. If it takes longer than the customary time frame, be sure you understand the reason given for the delay. It might also be a good idea to check with another shop that carries the same manufacturer to double check on production time.

When will you place the order for my dress? A 50 percent deposit is generally required to order wedding apparel. Once you make your deposit, your order should be placed with the manufacturer within a few working days. Some shops will hold your order for a period of time and this can increase the delivery time of your dress by several weeks or even months!

What will be the approximate ship date for my dress? Your dress is one of thousands that has to be produced. All manufacturers provide the shops with a ship date that is plus or minus a few days. It is important that you be aware of the ship date and be on the lookout for your dress as that day approaches. If that date is extended by several weeks, you may need to think about finding a new dress unless a good explanation can be given for the delay.

Does the manufacturer that produces my dress have a good quality assurance program? Like any other product, your wedding dress and bridesmaids' dresses should be examined for flaws before they leave the manufacturer. Some companies have much better quality control programs than others. Getting a dress that is free of flaws or can be turned around quickly, if there is a problem with it, will save you time and frustration.

What happens if the dress arrives from the manufacturer with a flaw in the material or a problem with the cut? A good company stands behind its product. The company should be able to turn a problem dress around within a reasonable time frame. Also, the problem dress should not be sent back until the new dress arrives in the shop to replace it. You do not want to be left without a dress as your wedding day approaches.

Will my dress need any alterations? Most wedding dresses will need some alterations for hem and bustle if it has a train. Depending upon where you fall on the manufacturer's size chart, more alterations may be necessary. You should ask to see the size chart before you place your order so that you will have a good picture of what will have to be done to the dress to get it to fit you well once it arrives from the manufacturer. The same rules apply to bridesmaids' dresses.

Do you have a seamstress in house to do any needed alterations? Most shops will have this service available or recommend a particular seamstress that you can work with. Remember that almost all wedding apparel will need some altering to fit right.

Is your seamstress a professional? It is very important that you get a positive answer here. Not all shops use a professional seamstress. Alterations are a different type of sewing and require the special skills of a professional. A non-professional or quasi-professional seamstress can ruin your garment.

Are the cost of alterations additional? Most bridal shops will require an additional fee to do any alterations. If the alterations are advertised as "free," the alteration expense will more than likely be represented somewhere in the initial cost of the garments. When alterations are advertised as free, corners are sometime cut to keep costly alterations in line. The results may be less than satisfactory.

What will the cost of alterations run? You should be able to get an estimate of the expense involved for the alterations of your wedding dress and the bridesmaids' dresses. Quality shops will post a general expense sheet. An average bridal hem will run about $30 to $60 and a bustle about the same. A bridesmaid's hem will run about $10. These figures will, of course, run more or less depending on the particular area where business is done.

What happens if there is a noticeable weight gain or loss after the order has been placed for my dress? A reputable bridal shop will measure you before your dress is ordered and, together with your input, decide from the manufacturer's size chart what size would come the closest to fitting you at the present time. If you gain or lose considerable weight, you will have to bear the consequences for excessive alterations to make the dress fit after it arrives in the shop.

A few dress companies will allow you to "restock" or replace a dress of one size for another if the dress and color that you have ordered are in stock. There is usually a "restocking" charge to the bridal shop, which will be passed on to you as the customer. This should be about $10 to $15.

How long does it take to get satin shoes and have them dyed? Most bridal shops sell and dye satin shoes. Shoes are usually in stock or can be obtained in a few working days from the various manufacturers. Shoes can be dyed and dried within a 24-hour period.

Can you redye some or all of the bridesmaids' previously used satin shoes?
Some satin shoes can be redyed if they are of a good quality to start with.
The less expensive ones are usually difficult to clean and redye because they
are made of a thinner material and can ripple across the toe area during a
redying process.

What accessories come with a tuxedo rental? A complete tuxedo includes
a shirt, jacket, pants, bow tie, and cummerbund or vest. Shoe rental is usually an extra charge.

How far in advance do we need to order the tuxes? Tuxedos are usually
booked several months in advance of the wedding to insure that you get the
style you want. Late spring, summer, and fall are the busiest times of the year
for tuxedo bookings. For winter weddings, tuxedos can usually be obtained
virtually anytime without the worry of availability of a particular style.

Can I get a good fitting tuxedo if I call or send the measurements in?
Good measurements mean a good fit, from wherever you get your tuxedos.
Quality shops will instruct you how to get good measurements if they are not
going to do the sizing themselves. It is a simple matter of measuring from
point A to point B over different areas of the body frame.

Knowing the height and weight of each person in your party also helps to
insure that the tuxedo will fit well. It is important to know if the person that
is going to use the tuxedo is athletic or muscular in nature. A very muscular
body build usually requires some special consideration to properly fit the
jacket and pants. A man with a large chest and a small waist will usually look
better in tails or a short jacket. Men with large thighs almost always require
one size up in pants from what they measure out at the waist.

Getting everyone dressed in the right apparel for your wedding ceremony
is like putting together a puzzle with many pieces. Taking all of this information into account will ease the process and help produce a less stressful shopping period and a more perfect outcome.

Chapter Four

"You Look Smashing!"

"I Don't Want to Look Like a Mother"

Formal dresses for the mothers of the bride and groom have a certain look to them. For many years now, the wedding industry has designed and produced the same type of apparel for mothers: The dresses are frequently designed with a draped effect, looking something along the lines of a toga with sleeves, and they are made of loose and flimsy material like georgette or chiffon. When these are pulled off the rack and shown to prospective mothers of the bridal couple, the mothers often remark, "This looks like something that my mother wore at my wedding!" If you have ever gone into a bridal shop or passed by and seen a motherly looking person running out of it, it is more than likely she has just been shown one of these dresses as a possibility for her son's or daughter's wedding!

Many mothers, like their sons and daughters, go to work each day outside of the home. Most of these busy, active women are in tune with fashion and are aware of what looks good in fashion, and what looks good on them. It is reasonable to understand their rejection of the chiffon-or-georgette-nightgown look that has been around for many generations. Thus, when one of her children is planning to be married, a mother wants to find an outfit designed with style and pizzazz that is flattering to her and makes her feel special also.

In the past several years, the industry has tried to accommodate mothers by giving their typical mother's-dress designs some shape, and by adding hoards of beading. The bead work usually causes the garment to retail for several hundred dollars, which many hard-working mothers find difficult to justify. Some of these dresses are pretty but are hardly something that a working mother can wear to another special occasion without looking like the mother of the bride all over again. Most, if not all, working mothers today say, "I want to find something that I can also use for other occasions after the wedding."

Another issue for mothers in choosing a dress is that they feel that they must complement the wedding party in some way. They are usually quite conscious of what color the bridesmaids will be wearing, so their outfit will "blend well with the wedding party." If this color is hard to find or not particularly flattering, a mother can have a difficult time finding the right dress.

The mother of the bride and groom usually faces a paradox of several dimensions. She needs to find an outfit that fits in with her contemporaries, complements the wedding party somewhat, can be worn to another occasion, and retails for less than one week's paycheck! This really does not seem like such a big order to fill at first look.

๛ What to Expect When You Start to Shop

Shopping for that special dress or outfit be an exasperating experience. As with brides' and bridesmaids' apparel, mothers' dresses are often cut from a small size chart. If you are normally a size 14, you can expect to suddenly become an 18 or more when trying on typical wedding apparel for mothers. The fun of shopping for that special dress for this important occasion can begin to dissipate as your focus turns to a crash diet.

If you are lucky enough to find a dress that you like, but have to order it from a sample to get your correct size and color, you should expect a waiting period of eight weeks or more with many designers. Not realizing this, many mothers do not allow enough time for ordering. You may find the perfect dress but not be able to get it in time for the wedding. (Jessica McClintock is one of the few companies that sells ready-wear bridal apparel for mothers and others. You can generally get one of her designs in a much shorter period of time, depending on availability of style, color, and size.)

Another problem that mothers frequently run into is finding the right outfit in the right color. Until recently, it seems that, just as black was once the designated color for women to wear to funerals, the pastel colors were designated for mothers at a wedding celebration. Many mothers now desire brighter colors because they look better and feel better in bright colors. They don't want to upstage the bride, but they also do not want to blend in with the wallpaper! Some of the more progressive and sensitive designers are starting to tune into this need and are using more color in their designs.

I have talked to mothers that have literally looked for weeks in several states and still not been able to find a suitable dress for the wedding because of these types of problems. As the date draws closer and closer, many women become very stressed over the matter of what they are going to wear. If you are a mother of the bride, it can be even more stressful because the mother of the groom usually waits to see what style and color you are going to use before searching out her own outfit.

✧ *Avoiding the Run Around*

Some mothers are turning to another mother for help. She is necessity, the mother of invention. There are several ideas that can be used to avoid the run around and frustration of seeing the same dresses over and over again in different shops, and knowing that they just will not work well for you.

If you have been out looking for a couple of weeks and have not been able to find a suitable outfit in a bridal shop, you probably should move on to other types of stores. Some mothers have better luck in the fancy dress section of a regular department store. These "out-of-the-loop"-type stores for wedding apparel can sometimes surprise you with the perfect dress. (Two companies that seem to produce many flattering designs in an assortment of bright pretty colors are After Dark and In The Mood.) A few quick phone calls to shops in your area can usually determine if there is anything of potential interest that should be investigated first.

Another possibility is to borrow an outfit from another mother who has already married off a child. If a friend or relative has a dress that you admire and it fits you and would work well for you at the wedding, why not consider this option? The same dress with different accessories will be hard to recognize on a different person. If it has been some time since the previous wedding, few people, if anyone, are going to remember it. Likewise, if it's a friend's dress and the wedding is being held far away, no one is going to know that your beautiful dress is borrowed.

If you have a dress that is flattering, why reinvent the wheel? Start with what you already have and what you know works well. One great idea is to take a dress that is already hanging in your closet and modify it to look different. The sleeves, belt, hemline, and other parts of the dress can be changed to give an old dress a new look, without altering the basic silhouette that flatters your figure. The color of the bridesmaids' dresses can be picked up in the material for a new set of sleeves or belt. A flounce or ruffle can be added on to the hemline, if the skirt is not too full. A bag of the same contrasting material can be made to go with the new additions to the dress. The leftover scraps of the new material can be used for a ribbon band or a flower embellishment for a hat, if you choose to wear one. A skirt can be taken off and added to a new top, or vice versa. All that is really required is a vivid imagination, some pretty new material, and a talented seamstress.

One mother who had looked for several weeks for a dress for her daughter's wedding ended up in a thrift shop and found "the perfect dress." In the better neighborhoods of all our cities, there are usually thrift shops that sell wonderful clothing that has sometimes hardly been worn. If you don't live close to this type of store, perhaps a friend or relative does and can scout things out for you. Sometimes you can do better in your own backyard. I once found a beautiful dress and evening cape for an occasion for which my husband and I wanted to look very special. The entire outfit cost me less than two dollars! I was almost embarrassed to accept all the compliments I received. No one suspected that I had obtained my outfit from a hospital thrift store in the small town next to our home.

⁓ Complementing the Wedding Party

It is the norm for most mothers of the bride and groom to try to find an outfit that matches the colors of the wedding party. This is not an absolute rule for all weddings, however, and some mothers have been known to deviate from this practice because they love a particular color or dress and feel good when wearing it. I dealt with one mother of the bride that fell in love with a red dress. The bride was going to use peach for her bridesmaids' dresses and I questioned these colors being used together. The mother followed her instincts and bought the red dress because it looked good on her and she felt good in it. People attending the wedding said that the mother of the bride looked absolutely beautiful, proving that mothers' dresses do not have to follow certain rules to fit in with the wedding party.

Another mother debated about wearing a certain dress that she loved. It was very flattering to her in many ways. The garment was heavily beaded and bought with her daughter's wedding in mind, off a discount rack, before the actual engagement. The mother of the groom, though, planned to wear a more conservative dress. This raised the question of the two mothers looking different from one another. "I love this dress and my daughter tells me to use it for her wedding because it looks so good on me. Will I look out of place next to the other mother?" She spent some time looking for a substitute dress with less glitter, but kept returning to her original choice. Instinct was telling her to go with her original selection and after many unsuccessful shopping trips, this mother followed her instincts and used the beaded dress.

One adroit friend of mine who is involved in the wedding business was once asked by a women who was about to assume this major role at her daughter's wedding, "What does the mother of the bride wear to the wedding?" "The mother of the bride can wear anything she wants to!" my friend replied. The point is that probably it is just as important to focus your attention on feeling good in your selected mother's dress as it is to blend in.

~ Designing the Perfect Dress for You

A relatively easy idea for obtaining the perfect dress, is to once again return to your clothing closet and focus on a particular dress or outfit that really looks nice on you. You have probably worn the poor thing to death because of this. You can take the outfit to a seamstress and have a new one custom designed, using your original as the model. It may seem like a difficult thing to accomplish, but there are many people who have the skills to do this for you. In many countries, this is how special clothing is made. In addition to being talented at sewing, a great seamstress will also have the skills required for pattern copy and design.

A wonderful and very talented woman who lives close to me can recreate just about anything on her sewing machine, with a sample model, or even just a picture to work from. She measures the client for size and also determines if any modifications are desired from the original design. She then instructs the client to obtain the correct amount of material of the desired type and color. With material in hand, she can produce a copy of an original in about two weeks time. Two to three fittings are required for this remarkable piece of work. Her fee is comparable to a modestly priced, factory-produced dress. With this method you can save a great deal of time and get a quality piece of clothing made to your exact specifications and color for the wedding.

To help you design your own dress or to modify an existing one, I have included some basic style silhouettes below (see Figure 4.1). You can use them by themselves, or mix and match to come up with the exact dress you are looking for but are unable to find in the size and color you need. By studying just a few basic silhouettes, you should be able to quickly hit upon a style that you are confident would look great on your figure. Use this knowledge to have the perfect dress made to order, or to guide you in shopping for your special-occasion apparel.

Figure 4.1
Basic Dress Styles

Dresses

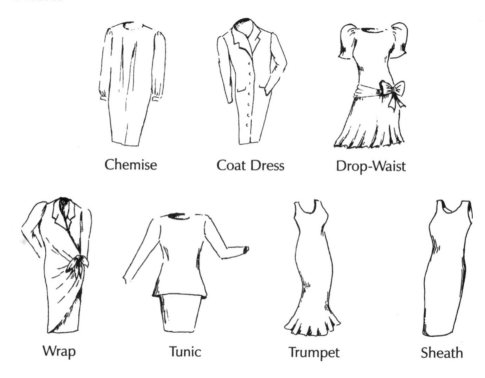

Chemise   Coat Dress   Drop-Waist

Wrap   Tunic   Trumpet   Sheath

Skirts

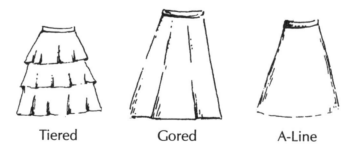

Tiered   Gored   A-Line

Blouses and Tops

Bolero   Chanel   Wrap

Peplum   Hacking   Blouson   Blazer

Chapter Five

Let Our Words Go Forth

Invitations and Announcements with Personal Pizzazz

✒ Using Desktop Publishing to Design Your Invitation

Using the services of a desktop publisher may be the answer for couples who cannot find an invitation they like or that is appropriate to the type of wedding service they plan to have. Desktop publishers can create a special accent or border for your card, drawing from a large library of available clip art designs. The various pieces of clip art and styles of print allow you to match your invitation to any wedding theme.

You act as the designer, using the computer skills of the publisher to create a card exactly the way you want it to be. A good desktop publisher can help you give shape and form to your invitation ideas in little more than an hour. A quick look through their clip art books and print styles will help you to decide if this is what you need to create your particular invitation.

If you decide to use the services of a desktop publisher to create your invitation, there is one important item you must attend to first. Before you can begin to create your invitation, you need to know where you can obtain envelopes and of what size. The size of the envelope should determine the dimensions of the invitation you want to create, not vice versa. Some couples have made the mistake of designing and printing their invitations first and then find it very difficult to locate envelopes to fit their invitation. This can become a time consuming, costly, and wasteful exercise. If you cannot find the correct size envelope for your invitation once it is designed and printed, you have the choice of cropping it to fit available envelopes or ordering specially sized envelopes. Often you must order these in boxes of one thousand, even though you only need one hundred. To prevent these problems, know ahead of time where you are going to get your envelopes, and then design your invitation to fit a size that is readily available.

A good place to obtain envelopes is through wedding invitation companies. Most invitation companies will sell just the envelopes for about 10¢ each and they can be ordered in increments of 25. You can order single or double envelopes. Envelopes with a colored liner to match your wedding colors are also available. The cost of this type of envelope will be more expensive, but it adds a nice finishing touch to the final design of your invitation.

A desktop publisher will take two to three working days to turn your design into a master that you can then use to print your invitations. The master may be produced as either a camera-ready piece of film that you would take to your printer, or a high quality printed paper that would allow you to have copies of your invitation made from a copying machine. I recommend that a printer be considered first for the job, as the time involved will be considerably less and the results of a higher quality.

If you decide to have your invitations made up at a copy center, check out more than one. Some use better equipment than others and this will affect the quality of your finished invitation. You will also have to give some thought to how many invitation can be copied onto one piece of paper, and the cutting and folding that will be needed to complete the job.

Exploring Other Creative Options

Some couples want to start from scratch and create their wedding invitation entirely themselves. If this is what you want to do, you need to get your envelops lined up first and then secure the paper stock on which your card will be printed. Most printers can order different types of paper in different weights, but the problem, once again, is that they usually have to order stock material in large quantities.

One place where you can purchase paper in small amounts is at an arts supply store or catalog. A stop at one of these stores, or a look through some of their catalogs will enable you to see many types of paper that could be used to create your invitation. (Call 1-800-A PAPERS for a free catalog from one of these companies to use in selecting your paper stock.) Once you have found the type of paper stock you like, you can experiment with different ways to personalize your invitation. When you get it the way you want it, you can take it to the printer for a professional printing job or make copies, using a copy machine. Again, you should carefully consider the pros and cons of each service for your particular wedding invitation.

✒ Original Invitation Ideas

Creating your distinct invitation will usually cost less than buying ones already designed from an invitation company. However, depending on the type of material and print job required, the cost can sometimes be much greater. Here are just a few ideas that other couples have used and some recreated samples of their invitations to help you design and create your own personal card.

One couple that was planning to have their wedding and reception at the oceanside in Maine simply went into a card shop and selected a pretty blank card with a picture scene on the front of it. The scene was of an ocean cottage, surrounded with flowers, and a path leading up to the cottage. Envelopes came with the cards so the task of finding envelopes was eliminated. They had a printer print a pretty verse on the little path leading up to the cottage, and then printed their invitation message on the inside of the card. This gave them a very personal wedding invitation and a beautiful reminder of their day.

Another couple bought some parchment paper with a pretty blue and rose floral border design on it and used this as the jacket for their invitation. Together, they designed a monogram for the center of the jacket. They then had the invitation printed in rose ink on a contrasting piece of plain parchment paper. When the two pieces of paper were placed together and folded in half, a thin rose colored ribbon was tied around the center, with a small bow displayed at the top outside corner of the card. "Corner copy," or a small note, usually printed on the lower left hand corner of the invitation, told of the reception to follow. The reply cards were done on a heavier piece of paper stock and cropped to fit the small return envelope. Figure 5.1 shows a recreated sample of this type of invitation.

Figure 5.1
Sample Invitation

Another bride used a heavy paper, called index stock, to create her invitations, and included a direction card on the back. She decorated each invitation with original hand-painted art work after they were printed. She also did a reply card in the same style.

> I started making our invitations several months before the date that they were due to be mailed, to allow enough time to complete my project without feeling rushed. I hand painted just a few cards each night to keep the work interesting and fun. It was something I could do while listening to music or watching a TV program. It was really a lot of fun and made us actually feel that we were accomplishing something on our wedding plans each day. Getting the envelopes was probably the most difficult part for me because I didn't think this through beforehand.

An actual sample of this creative invitation is shown in Figure 5.2. (The reply card sample is not shown. It was designed with some of the same art work, but this card was only 3-½" by 2-½" in size to fit the size of the reply envelope.)

Figure 5.2
Sample Invitation B
Front of Invitation

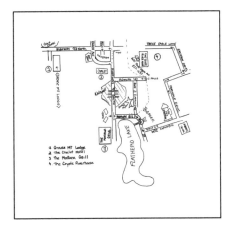

Figure 5.2 (continued)
Back of Invitation with Directions to Wedding

❧ Wedding Scrolls and Programs

You can also design and produce your own scrolls and wedding programs in the same fashion. Look for thin types of paper for the scrolls, such as onion skin, rice paper, or parchment. You can print up your thank-you message on a home computer using your special paper or have a professional printer do the job for you. After rolling up the scrolls, secure each one with a small ribbon, using the color theme of your wedding, of course (see Figure 5.3).

Figure 5.3
Wedding Scroll

The prophet and poet Kahilil Gibran had some elegant words about marriage which could be used in whole or in part for the message on your wedding scrolls.

Marriage is the union of two divinities
that a third might be born on earth.
It is the union of two souls in a strong love
for the abolishment of separteness.
It is that higher unity which fuses the separate unities
within the two spirits.
It is the golden ring in a chain whose beginning is a glance,
and whose ending is Eternity.
It is the pure rain that falls from an unblemished sky to fructify
and bless the fields of divine Nature.
As the first glance from the eyes of the beloved
is like a seed sown in the human heart,
and the first kiss of her lips like a flower
upon the branch of the Tree of Life,
So the union of two lovers in marriage
is like the first fruit of the first flower of that seed.

Thank You for Sharing With Us
The First Day of Our New Life Together
Melody and Jon
June 16, 1993

The Voice of the Master by Kahlil Gibran

There is also this beautiful verse from 1st Corinthians, Chapter 13, Verses 4-8, that could be used in whole or in part for your thank you scrolls.

Love is patient; and kind.
Love is not jealous,
it does not put on airs,
it is not snobbish.
Love is never rude,
it is not self-seeking,
it is not prone to anger;
neither does it brood over injuries.
Love does not rejoice in what is wrong

but rejoices with the truth.
There is no limit to love's forbearance,
to its trust,
its hope,
its power to endure.
Love never fails.

Thank you for Sharing this Precious Day with Us
Amanda and Ray
May 20, 1994

The New American Bible 1971-72 edition (Catholic)

Love is patient; love is kind and envies no one. Love is never boastful, nor conceited, nor rude; never selfish, not quick to take offense. Love keeps no score of wrongs; does not gloat over other men's sins, but delights in the truth. There is nothing love cannot face; there is no limit to its faith, its hope, and its endurance. Love will never come to an end.

1 Corinthians 13:4-8 (The New English Bible)

You can create your own wedding programs using different or unusual types of paper on which to print your information. Regular weight paper can be used, or you could use cover stock if you want something with more weight . You can design your programs using 8-½" by11" paper stock, so they simply fold in half, or use the tri-fold method where you end up with three columns of type on one page of paper. See the examples in Figure 5.4.

Figure 5.4
Sample Folds for Wedding Programs

 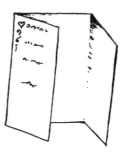

Regular Fold Program   Tri-Fold Program

The information for your wedding program should include everything that will take place during the ceremony and a list of your participants. Program content may differ according to the customs of each religious sect. The officiator performing your service will be able to offer guidance in this regard. Many ministers encourage couples to select or add their own music and readings. An example of wedding program wording done on a tri-fold paper is shown in Figure 5.5:

Figure 5.5
Sample of Wedding Program

Our Marriage Ceremony

Sabrina Canales
&
Gregory F. Smith

Front of Program

The Marriage Service of
Sabrina Canales
&
Gregory F. Smith

Saturday,
the seventh of June, 1995
LaVillita Church
San Antonio, Texas
4:00 p.m.

Prelude Music

Ode To Joy	Beethoven
Barcarolle	Offenbach
Romance	Sibelius

Lighting of Candles

Solo

| Follow Me | John Denver |

Processional

| Trumpet Voluntary | Purcell |

Marriage Service

Prayer
Readings
Hymn
Promises
Exchange of Vows and Rings
Blessing
Lighting of Unity Candle

Solo

| The Rose | Franderic Forrest |

Prayers
Benediction

Recessional

| Wedding March | Mendelssohn |

Pastor
Organist
Vocalist
Reader

The Wedding Party

Maid of Honor
Bridesmaids
Best Man
Groomsmen
Flower Girl
Ring Bearer
Ushers
Candle Lighters
Bride's Parents
Groom's Parents

"The path that leads to
happiness is so narrow
that two cannot walk on
it, unless they become
one."

| Left Inside Page | Middle Inside Page | Right Inside Page |

☙ Preserving Your Invitation in Marble, Pewter, and Mirrors

Your wedding invitation represents a part of your marriage history. Probably a sizable amount of time and effort was involved in its selection and composition. Having a beautiful way of preserving and displaying it after the wedding is important.

There are many ways to preserve your wedding invitation so that you can display it in your home. Three of the most beautiful and effective methods that I have recently seen are having your invitation reproduced on a piece of Vermont Marble, enclosing a copy of the original invitation in an especially handsome pewter frame, or designing a hall mirror that also acts as a display case for your card.

Vermont Stoneworks, located beside the green on Main Street in Chester, Vermont, can reproduce an exact copy of any wedding invitation on a piece of Vermont marble. The artist uses a special laser engraving process to engraved the marble with gold ink. The engraving process also captures any detailed artwork that is on the original card, so the entire invitation is duplicated onto the marble. Different colored marble is used, according to the customer's preference. White, black, and green marble are among the more popular. Two sizes are offered, 4" by 7" and 6" by 10". The price is about $40 to $60, depending on the size of reproduction you desire.

The marble invitation makes a nice gift for any couple, whether it is a gift to themselves or one given to them by a family member or wedding guest. It can be used in several ways. It can be displayed on a fireplace mantle or table when set into a small holder that can also be ordered with the reproduction piece The marble invitation can be used to simply set your wedding toast glasses on, wherever these are set out in your home. All that is needed to have the reproduction done is an actual invitation. The turn around time is about one week.

Another wonderful idea for preserving your invitation is to frame it in fine pewter. There are several companies that produce pewter frames but Seagull Pewter of Pugwash, Nova Scotia, produces exceptionally beautiful ones. They have several pewter frames with wedding motifs and wedding themes, such as bells and doves, and others with different types of flowers and details that are engraved into the pewter itself. When you encase your card within these lovely pewter borders, your wedding invitation becomes an unforgettable and priceless family heirloom to grace your home.

One couple that put a great deal of thought and effort into designing a personal invitation had a mirror cut to a specific size and bordered with a wood frame. At the top of the mirror, the wood frame was extended to allow a space for their invitation. The picture front and inside message of the card was "matted" and then enclosed within the glass covered, wooden-framed space above the mirror. "This made a wonderful decoration for our home and we get to see our invitation each day as we go off to work. It's a great reminder of our wedding day for us and everyone who visits our home." You can design your own invitation mirror!

Chapter 6

Take One—Lights, Camera, Action!

Capturing Your Wedding Day History in Multiple Mediums

Of the many things that need to be arranged for your wedding day, probably none is more important than having a great photographer, so you can remember the event when it is all over. As the old saying goes, "a picture is worth a thousand words." Having members of your family and friends gathered together in one place gives you the opportunity to collect precious photos that will tell the stories of your lives in miniature to future generations. Using a professional photographer in some capacity is an absolute must for any couple, regardless of their wedding budget. The trained eye, timing, and sophisticated equipment of a professional will enable you to remember with absolute clarity the people, details, and feelings that permeated your special day.

❧ Creative Professional Photography

When you set out to select your professional photographer, you should look for several things to get quality, creative photos. The type of equipment and the type of film used, and the skill and ability of the person you select to capture your wedding day history in photography will determine the quality, intensity, and creativity of your pictures.

To get pictures that have a deeper tone and feeling, much will depend on the type of lighting the photographer uses. The strobe light or the flash units attached to a professional's camera are the key to good lighting and wonderfully alive pictures. The use of several strobes, at least three, will give a "modeling," or three-dimensional, effect, which will add depth and contour to the finished photo. The subjects in the picture will appear more alive and animated. The use of one strobe light, giving light to the front of the picture only, will make your photos appear flat and less alive because of the dark shadows around the subject. Be sure that your photographer plans to use several strobes to shoot your wedding pictures.

The type of film used is also very important. Thirty-five millimeter film will not produce quality enlargements of your wedding pictures because the resulting negative is too small. When photos are enlarged using small negatives, they appear grainy and color resolution is lost. The use of 120 millimeter film will result in better overall sharpness and depth of color in both small and enlarged pictures. Color will fade from all pictures over a period of time. More lasting color is possible when 120 millimeter film is used from the beginning.

The ability to pose the subjects with creative imagination is a gift to some and carefully learned by others. Having a photographer that skillfully uses multiple posing techniques will add grace, humor, and radiance to your wedding photography.

Always inquire about whose work you are looking at when reviewing samples, and who will actually be shooting your wedding. In some cases, the work that you review in the photographer's studio may not be that of the person who will be assigned to your wedding. Some studios may hire a "traveling fireman" to carry the extra work of the day. If this is the case, ask to see that person's work.

Two other important questions should be raised when you are selecting a professional wedding photographer:

1. *Who will do the job if your photographer becomes ill on or before your wedding day?* You should ask to review some of the work of anyone who would cover your wedding in a case such as this.

2. *Does the photographer carry insurance?* Your wedding day film will be sent off to a laboratory to be developed. Once the film leaves the hands of the studio, problems that can occur in transit or within the laboratory itself, are out of the photographer's control. If something should happen to your film somewhere along the line, and the photographer does not carry insurance, you may not only lose out on your pictures but also the money you have invested in them.

Taking these few items into consideration will help you to review the photographer's work with a sharp eye, and to ask knowledgeable questions to better select a photographer who will produce the best quality pictures of your wedding day.

⇜ Creative Posing for Your Wedding Pictures

Posing one or more persons for a photograph is something like arranging flowers in a vase. How they are oriented to one another and to the vase alone or collectively sends a message to the viewer. There are three types of poses for pictures and each presents a different message. When all three are included in your wedding photography, your wedding album will appear more creative.

Traditional Posing

Traditional posings are pictures of an individual or group of people together. These are probably the least time consuming and easiest to shoot for the professional photographer and amateur alike. If you look back into your parents' wedding albums, you will probably find many, if not all, of their poses were traditional. This type of posing requires that you stand or sit up straight and "say cheese!" While these pictures are important to any wedding album, traditional poses alone are unable to tell in depth the full story of what took place that day. To capture this, other types of posing are needed.

Illustrative

This type of posing includes background information along with the main subjects. The church where you were just married, the horse and buggy that you are about to ride in, or a beautiful flower garden at the place of your reception fall into this category. In addition to the beautiful bride and handsome groom, illustrative poses provide interesting information for the viewer to contemplate because they tell a little more about the environment that surrounded you during the wedding.

Fashion

This type of posing produces pictures that catch your eye and hold your attention because they are stylish and unconventional. Bold and unusual fashion-magazine poses draw your attention into the picture because of this. One bride recently told of her plan to include her pony in several of her wedding photos. "I'm going to dress him up with a hat full of flowers and do a nose to nose shot with him in his hat and me in my wedding dress!" Fashion poses in your wedding album give a jazzy tone to your overall story.

⊱ Creative Wedding Photos to Consider

If you take the time to work with your photographer and carefully plan out the type of wedding pictures you want to create, using his or her talent and ability, your wedding photography will be personal and evoke detailed memories. Here are just a few creative ideas to ask about.

A close-up shot of the bridal bouquet. A picture of your wedding bouquet alone will make a wonderful "historical" still-life to brighten any wall of your home if you have it enlarged to a 16" by 24". Brides are using bold colors in their flowers now and these arrangements make great pictures to enlarge, to use for interior decoration of your living space. If it rains on your wedding day, a close up shot of your bouquet taken with some raindrops on the flowers will look like the kiss of dew on the petals.

A beautiful special effect that can be done with a certain lens attachment is vignetting. In this photo, a bold center, or main focus, is framed by toning down the outer edges in a soft blur. The contrast of the soft blurs of the photo's edges and the sharply detailed image of the main focus, such as a face or a flower, will give your picture a misty effect. When vignetting is used for a picture of the bride or bride and groom together, the face and eyes will be sharply detailed, picking up the emotions of the day.

If your wedding is to take place at sunrise or sunset, think about having your photographer use a telephoto lens to capture a sun or moon that can be enlarged, and have him place your silhouettes against it. This type of picture dramatically depicts that the time of day or night when your marriage occurred was special.

A great montage photo can be created when a picture of the bride and groom is spliced together with a picture of each from another very special time in your lives, that being the joyful childhood years.

If your wedding day forecast is for rain or snow, ask to have some weather photos done to capture the essence of your wedding day weather on film. Think about a water reflection picture of the bride and groom, using a nearby puddle or body of water. Or have your attendants build you a wedding snowperson and then step into the scene for some imaginative pictures of the two of you completing the task in your wedding finery.

The snowperson can even be colored using a mixture of cake coloring and water to bring your wedding colors into the picture if you desire. Have your attendants color your snowperson using this mixture and a plastic spray bottle.

What about a fun picture of the happily married couple "dancing in the rain" at the end of the celebration? Your wedding clothes are going to have to be cleaned anyway. Why not splash around some to capture the feeling of your marriage bliss, in spite of the weather? If the sun is out, get a shadow photo. The elements on the day of your marriage, whatever they are, can be captured in some way by your photographer.

An illustrative wedding picture that is wonderful to have in your album is one with your family home in the background. The home where you grew up, quietly standing behind you, will give you an unexpected treasure to reflect on as the years pass. You'll be glad that you captured a photo of this special time at this special place. This is especially true if your home was a place of great joy and happiness. This type of background information links one important passage of time with another and provides visual roots for your future family. When the photographer uses selective focusing, so that the home background is slightly out of focus, in contrast to a very sharp picture of the bride and groom, this picture speaks in soft whispers of endings and new beginnings.

A close-up of your empty wedding shoes, posed side by side in just the right way, perhaps propped up on the ring pillow, tells a tacit story of the walk down the aisle, the waiting at the front of the church, the reception dances, and the walking together that you will do throughout your married lives. An enlargement of this picture would make a focal point and conversational piece in any room in your home.

Pictures that can often be overlooked at wedding scenes are families within your families. With so many wonderful relatives gathered together in one place, and dressed in their finest, do not overlook having group pictures taken of each family during any of the photographer's "down time" at your wedding. These photos represent your roots on both sides of your families. They make wonderful photos for your home or as a gift to those families at a later time.

Ask your photographer about using a matte box accessory for the lens to shoot a picture that will give you a double exposure or divided picture such as the steeple of the church and the bride and groom in one photo.

A star filter will give the candle lights or other small lights at your ceremony a magical and romantic twinkle or star burst effect in your photos and sprinkle a little stardust into your wedding album. As many as eight star bursts on one point of light can be obtained with different filters.

A sepia-toned picture, or a photo that gives the appearance of an old tintype photo, makes the perfect picture for an antique frame and a focal point on any mantle or table in your home. Likewise, black and white pictures add intensity, a sense of timelessness, and mystery to photography. They also will not fade in color tone over time.

Finally, a couple of sequencing frames that capture a very slight change of eye focus or body position can produce a mini-story within the overall narrative of your photo album.

A New Trend

A new trend in professional wedding photography is to shoot many of the couple's and their attendants' photos before the ceremony. The rationale for setting aside the old superstition of the groom's not seeing the bride before the ceremony is changing for many reasons. One is that, in this way, the bride and groom are among the first to see each other on this special day. Some couples feel less nervous during the marriage ceremony when an hour or so is spent together prior to the ceremony. The vows and other words spoken during their ceremony can be more readily absorbed and remembered when some of the anxieties are quelled beforehand. Also, the photography time does not cut into the party time following the ceremony.

Creative Candid Shots

This is the area where you can employ the services of that friend or relative that is a photography buff. In addition to the professional photographer, request that this particular friend or relative be armed with his or her camera and a supply of film, to take candid shots of all the activity throughout the day. Give this person a list of the particular shots you would like him or her to take, so that in all the excitement of the day nothing is overlooked.

Pictures of the building and grounds where the wedding and reception took place are often overlooked and under shot. They too are important if you want to have total recall of your wedding activities as the years pass. A picture of the name of the church, inn, or marriage site should be taken as a document of where all this activity actually occurred.

One bride and groom requested that a picture be taken of each couple attending their wedding so they could include pictures of their guests enjoying their wedding with their thank-you notes. Another bride and groom who were married at a beautiful and historical chapel in the month of May when it was engulfed with flowering trees and shrubs, requested that the friend assigned to take candid pictures during their wedding concentrate much of his efforts on the chapel itself. They wanted to have an artist do a watercolor of the scene and intended to give him one of the candid shots to work from.

One very imaginative couple instructed the assigned "candid camera" relative to take close up pictures of all the tiny details that were part of their wedding day. They gave this person a list of items, such as the lace on the bride's gown, the boutonniere on the lapel of the groom's tuxedo, the toasting glasses, the decoration on the bride's shoes, the gifts that the couple gave to their wedding party, the ring pillow, the favors, the bridesmaids' flowers against the satin of their dresses, the marriage certificate, and the "just married" sign attached to the bumper of the wedding car. They wanted to use these types of pictures, of their wedding details and memories, as an abstract border around a planned silhouette shot of them dancing at the reception.

⊷ Wedding Videos

Almost all couples getting married today want a video of their wedding and reception, and those who omit it often wish as time passes that they had one made. Using professionals to do your work is highly recommended. Their equipment is usually much more sophisticated than that of a relative or friend, so that the resolution or clarity of your tape will be of higher quality. Copies can then be made of your original tape without the loss of clarity and color that occurs when the original tape is made with an average camcorder and film. Probably most important, it frees up relatives or friends to partake of the wedding festivities.

If you plan to have a "homemade tape" done of your wedding, consider having professionals edit your tapes into a single one that is polished and shows the major points of your wedding in an abridged time frame. Before you contract for their services, ask about the type of equipment used and the amount of color and clarity change that might occur to your tape. Again be sure to instruct the person shooting your original tape to get footage of the names of the marriage site and reception place for a lasting record of where it all took place.

❧ *Montage Video*

You can have a short tape produced by editing out of the original tape of your wedding several special moments that stand alone because of the deep emotions they evoke. A montage, or freeze frame, video allows you to make time stand still while you reflect on these most special moments in your lives. The best of the best from your original videotape can be selected for a montage video, to give you a short but vivid recall of your wedding day.

Freeze frame videos can also be put together using the negatives of still pictures from your wedding, if you did not have a video made at the time. Placing them in proper sequence and adding beautiful background music organizes your wedding story and allows the emotions and elegance of your day to be felt more deeply through your pictures, projected onto the large screen. Freeze frame videos are shorter because they are of just the high-lights of your wedding and can be watched with ease while you are doing other things around the house. A two and one half hour wedding tape can be abridged into a twenty minute montage video that lends itself to better viewing when friends and relatives stop to visit and you are itching to show your video again.

Adding music to your tape makes it come alive with the emotions and feelings of that day. Much of the music from earlier times focused on love and romance. There were many beautiful melodies and lyrics written during the fifties that blend especially well with wedding scenes. "To the Aisle" by The Five Saturns is one piece that captures and epitomizes the feelings of your wedding day and follows the sequence of love and romance that led you to the crossroad and ceremony of marriage.

✒ *Audiopictures*®

During the nineteenth century, a Russian composer and artist named Mussorgsky, used a musical score to accompany a showing of artwork. He wrote instrumental pieces of music to accompany the drawings to express, in musical tones, the meaning that had been captured in oil on the canvas. The result was a kind of talking picture, which one could not only look at, but also hear. Another composer, Sir Arthur Bliss, produced a symphony entitled Color Symphony, by writing musical interpretations of certain groups of colors. The intonations and feeling of his music depicted purple as pageantry, red as wine, blue as deep water, and for the color green, the sound and feeling of hope.

An imaginative, contemporary couple, Marcia Phillips and John Lovejoy of Claremont, New Hampshire, have taken the logic of these previous artists and come up with a wonderful new idea to quicken your sense of sight and sound. It is called an Audiopicture®. An Audiopicture® stimulates pleasurable memories by combining a special picture with special music.

Phillips, an innovative photographer, conveys a mood interpretation of a specific picture to Lovejoy who is a musician and composer. He then writes a music score to accompany the photograph. The result is a beautiful image, fused together with lovely music that expresses the content of that image.

"The visual expression of the picture is brought to life by an original music score. Audiopictures® are a new kind of art expression. Some people feel that they are literally taken back in time to that special place in the picture, through this imaginative and creative process. It is something like having your own minisymphony, inspired by a personal, meaningful picture."

The Audiopictures® are used to decorate and beautify a living space with a timeless remembrance of a certain place and moment in your lives. A visual image of this picture stays with you while listening to the musical interpretation. Pictures of two wedding sites in New Hampshire are illustrated here, and also a picture of a hot air balloon, which has been a magical wedding site for some couples (see Figure 6.1). The types of musical impressions associated with each are explained. This new concept of visual and musical expression can be further explored for your wedding site by contacting the artists directly at 1-603-542-8583.

Figure 6.1
Sample Audiopictures®

Gateway to Monadnock

This music brings movement to the quiet majesty of this great mountain. Orchestration was important here, using such powerful instruments as horns, organ and tympani. There is also a more delicate side to this audiopicture, beckoning one to come through the gate to another world.

Balloon

This Audiopicture gives "rise" (!) to the feeling of ultimate freedom and weightlessness. Sound effects of escaping gas put the listener in the canopy and let the imagination go from there.

The Birches

The theme for this picture is twofold. Initially, a peaceful, reflective tone catches the listener's ears, giving the feeling of strolling through the birches on a warm summer day. The second theme focuses more on the majesty of the sun as it peeks through the trees and into the open field beyond. Collectively, the music sets a tone of calm and inner peace.

✒ Stone Reproductions of Wedding Scenes

If you want memories of your wedding day chiseled in stone, I direct you once again to Vermont Stoneworks, of Chester, Vermont. Taking a picture of some part of your wedding that you particularly love, the artist here can use a laser to cut the impression of it into a piece of Vermont marble or stone.

One couple had a replication of the chapel where they were married done this way, and they display it along with their wedding pictures. It could also be used to make a very meaningful center stone for your fireplace hearth or become part of the walk that is the entrance to your home. You can reach Stoneworks at 1-802-875-4141 or 1-802-875-4004.

Chapter Seven

Modest Income Designs

Spinning Hay Into Gold—La Creative Embellishment

Most couples planning a wedding do not have unlimited financial resources. Some may simply choose to scale down the wedding ceremony to save their funds for another important element of their married lives, such as a longer, more elaborate honeymoon, or perhaps they are considering a downpayment on their first home. Others may have friends on a tight budget that cannot afford a large outlay of cash to be in their wedding, or may themselves have limited funds. In any case, a beautiful wedding is still possible, even with a modest budget, if you plan carefully and shop around for your needs and services. You can concentrate your efforts in a direction that will help you to save money but still design an elegant and memorable wedding.

One of the first places to start is to plan your wedding for an off-season month. Just like most businesses, the wedding business is seasonal. If you plan your wedding for one of the off-season months, you will be able to bargain for almost everything you need and get a much better deal than when hundreds of other couples are lining up to do business. November through January are generally considered the slow months for weddings. Wedding apparel shops are hungry for business during this time.

Tuxedo companies usually drop their rental fees dramatically during the month of December. Some companies will reduce the price of their tuxedo rentals if they are booked during the off-season months for a future wedding date. Bridal shops often advertise sales of their wedding dress samples for as much as 60 percent off the regular retail prices during these months, to prepare for incoming inventory. Even if a sale is not advertised, simply asking the shop owner about reduced pricing on discontinued samples of wedding apparel can be worthwhile. If you are open to different styles and materials, you should be able to acquire all of your wedding apparel needs at reduced prices using the window of an "off season" to make your purchases.

✎ How to Look Expensive

Another way to acquire expensive-looking wedding apparel is to begin with a relatively simple item, such as a very plain wedding dress, and embellish it. Lace appliqués, pearl beading, and sequins are relatively inexpensive when they are purchased separately and then applied by hand. Lace and beading around the hem of a wedding dress always make it look more lavish than one without this feature. The T. R. Thornton Wedding Apparel Company, located in Belton, Texas, produces a basic wedding dress for this very reason. You can purchase the dress alone and add your creative ideas to embellish it, or buy it with optional lace trim that you then apply to the dress, using the directions that come with a lace trim kit.

An easy and relatively inexpensive method of acquiring a pretty wedding dress is to purchase a basic bridesmaid's dress in white or ivory, and use it as a wedding dress by enhancing the garment with lace, beads and sequins, or by adding a long detachable train. A cathedral length veil can also be added to a headpiece to add a touch of elegance to a plain, floor-length, white or ivory bridesmaid's dress. Veiling is relatively inexpensive and can make a simple wedding dress look quite lavish.

If you are able to sew and can plan far in advance, making your wedding apparel is one way to substantially reduce this wedding expense. If you do not know how to sew, you can enroll yourself in a sewing class and make your wedding dress as your class project. You will not only save a great deal of money, but acquire skills that will come in handy for decorating a home and sewing family clothing later on. Having a teacher available to guide you will insure a quality, finished piece of wedding apparel. Making a wedding dress with a detachable train will make your project even easier because it will lessen the amount of material you have to contend with on the machine as you start your project. Sewing is not difficult once you acquire some direction from a qualified sewing teacher and if you allow yourself ample time to do a good job of completing your project.

If you have a relative or friend who is a good seamstress and able to discipline his or her time well, you might inquire about hiring that person to make your wedding apparel. The important thing with any of these ideas is to always allow yourself enough time to get satisfactory results for your wedding day.

❧ Working with What Is Available

There are over two million weddings each year in the United States alone, and the apparel used in these weddings is hanging in closets all over the land. If you are on a tight budget and trying to realize ways to cut the cost of your wedding apparel needs, why not consider recycling previously worn apparel for yourself or your bridesmaids?

One bride who attended a friend's wedding, several months before her own, liked the color and style of the bridesmaids' dresses. She simply asked each bridesmaid if she could buy their dress for use in her upcoming wedding. They struck a bargain and the dresses were exchanged for very little money. She acquired her five bridesmaids' dresses for less than the price of one new one. Many bridesmaids' dresses are hung in closets, never to see the light of day again. These particular bridesmaids were happy to accommodate this bride with the sale of their dresses, to recoup some money on a dress that they knew they would never use again.

The bride realized the various size dresses could all be made to fit her attendants with little effort. With the exception of her friend who was being married that day, none of the other people present would attend her wedding. To her own family and friends, the dresses would appear to be new. She built her color scheme around them. This smart and savvy bride concluded that using different bridesmaids and flowers, would modify the dresses and make them look fresh and new for her wedding. She had acquired beautiful bridesmaids' dresses by recycling what was already available and, in the process, drastically reduced the cost of her bridesmaids' apparel for her friends who were to be in her wedding.

Previously worn bridesmaids' dresses can also be altered to take on different look. Think about raising or lowering the hemline and changing the look of the sleeve to give the dress an entirely new appearance. A separate underskirt with an elasticized waist, made of different fabric or a contrasting color, can easily be added to make a short skirt long. Add a new cuff to the sleeve using this same material to tie the upper part of the dress in with the new skirt. This will create a new and different, recycled bridesmaid's dress. If you like the basic design of a previously worn bridesmaid dress, think about how making a few minor additions can change the dress to make it look fresh and new again.

One bridesmaid that I recently worked with planned to use a recycled dress, but was concerned because of some scarring on one of her upper arms. The dress she wanted to use had short sleeves that exposed the areas on her arms she wished to have covered. The sleeves were able to be lengthened somewhat by removing two small bows from the back of the dress and attaching them to the lower end of each sleeve. I then suggested she buy a pair of opera-length dyeable gloves, dyed to match the dress color. Dyeable gloves are made of a special fabric that will absorb dye coloring, and they come in several styles and length. Most bridal shops carry them or can easily obtain them. I also suggested that the gloves be fingerless to make them more functional. Her hands would be free to eat, so she would not have to remove them during the meal. With these small alterations, her scarred arm was completely covered, and she had a stylish dress that looked entirely different from that with which she started out.

✎ Using Your Mother's Wedding Dress

Many a mother has a secret wish that her daughter will choose to be married in the wedding dress in which she was married. The reality is that fewer than 4 percent of brides elect to reuse their mother's wedding dress, for a number of reasons. If the dress was not packed away in an airtight place, like a cedar chest or specially preserved in an airtight box, it may have become discolored. A white dress not properly preserved will look ivory in color twenty years later. If the dress was not cleaned immediately following the wedding, there may be spots that are now impossible to have removed. The dress also simply may not be the right size or style.

If you really want to use your mother's wedding dress, or another one that has been passed down to you, all of these problems can be overcome. The dress size can be increased by letting seams out or using material from the train, if it has one, to enlarge the dress bodice and sleeves. Small soiled areas left on the dress from the original wearing can often be concealed by covering them with new lace appliqués that closely match the lace already on the dress. All of the lace embellishments can be removed and completely redone with new beading and sequins, if desired. If the dress has yellowed, it is now very much in style. More and more brides are choosing ivory wedding dresses because of their romantic, antique appearance. Many of the older wedding dresses were also made of better quality materials than those used for contemporary dresses. So if there is a wedding dress up in the attic of your parents' home and your wedding budget is limited, check it out before you set out to buy a new one. You may be pleasantly surprised to find a true gem obscurely packed away from view.

❧ Renting and Borrowing—It Can Be Done!

Although men have been renting tuxedoes for many years, it was only recently that the idea of women's renting dresses to wear on special occasions caught on. Rental companies for women's apparel are usually located in metropolitan areas. There are two national companies that have been renting women's wedding apparel for several years now and they will ship their rentals anywhere. These are Tux Town and Classic Collection, located in Bountiful, Utah, and Jandi Rentals of Knoxville, Tennessee.

Each company has several styles and colors of bridesmaids' dresses and wedding dresses that they sublet to bridal shops for rental wear. The dresses can be selected and rented through a catalogue display. Also, you can usually have a dress shipped to you for preview for a small sum. Rental fees will vary, but they usually amount to one-half or less of the full retail price of a new dress. The biggest drawback of rental dresses is that you will not have them until the week of your wedding. If your bridesmaids are average sizes, this should not present a problem when the dresses are ordered according to accurate measurements. If you or one of your bridesmaids is difficult to fit, rental dresses can sometimes present a problem, as alterations must be kept to a minimum. Nevertheless, special occasion rental dresses should not be ruled out until you have investigated this option and know what is available to you. The telephone numbers for each company are Tux Town and Classic Collection, 1-800-824-0047, and Jandy Rentals, 1-800-342-1544.

❧ "Something Borrowed . . ."

Borrowing wedding apparel is something that used to be done routinely with great success. I personally borrowed my headpiece and veil from my sister-in-law when I set out to buy my own and realized how expensive this purchase was going to be. Most people will be flattered that you want to use a piece of their wedding apparel and accommodate you. One of my best friends was married in a borrowed wedding dress and no one ever knew the difference. Her mother had been to a beautiful wedding of a friend's daughter and admired the wedding dress. The bride was the same size as her daughter. The mother simply asked her good friend if the dress could be borrowed for her own daughter's wedding. During the fifties, this was not an uncommon occurrence. People tried to live within their means and often helped each other out whenever necessary. If you need to cut corners, and know of a beautiful dress that begs to be worn, investigate borrowing it for your wedding. You can choose to tell or not tell others about your wonderful find.

✎ Let Nature and Others Do the Decorating

Depending on where you live, where you plan to be married, and the time of year, your wedding site can be decorated by nature. If you are planning to have a home reception, think about the time of year when the yard is the most in bloom to add nature's touch to the festivities of your wedding day. Lilac bushes and flowering trees make graceful and elegant additions for beautiful wedding ceremonies and receptions. Beautiful and graceful Bridal Wreath is a white flowering shrub found in spring, and its small, delicate, and graceful flowers have a pretty scent. This shrub makes a great natural enhancer to any spring wedding scene.

For Christian couples, getting married during the December season is a practical way to have your wedding scene decorations done scot-free. Churches and reception sites are already decorated with greens and flowers several weeks before and after Christmas day. The beauty of the festive holiday season spills easily over into a wedding theme. What better gift to give to each other and your families during this special time of year than your marriage. A wedding ceremony and celebration party on New Year's Eve gives everyone a wonderful event to look forward to and even more of a reason to celebrate. The celebratory atmosphere already exists and is just waiting for you to plan your marriage ceremony and celebration party!

✎ Make Your Own Music

Several music companies are now providing music on tapes that are designed for sing-along. American Accompaniment Track Tapes of Nashville, Tennessee (phone 1-800-525-7155) produces many sound tracks of popular music for all occasions, including weddings. The voice has been removed from original track music, so that someone who likes to sing can have a professional musical accompaniment, without the expense of an instrumental group. Using their "wedding song cassettes" along with someone who can sing well can lower the cost of your ceremony music. These tapes and others combined with a good tape player can also be used to provide the musical entertainment for your celebration party. Assigning each person in your wedding party a short segment of time to be your "disc jockey" can dramatically reduce this music expense.

❧ Small, Romantic, and Intimate—A Great Way Out for Some

For couples who are really finding it difficult to come up with the amount of funds necessary for a large wedding, or have a family that is fragmented and difficult to get together, it is probably better to turn their thoughts in the opposite direction. A small wedding is much easier to control in every way and it can be made just as beautiful and memorable. Often times, a small wedding scene is more meaningful for everyone involved, especially if each invited guest can somehow take an active part in the ceremony. In this regard, a small wedding can perhaps better hone in on what marriage is truly all about.

A small wedding may better meet the needs of a couple that have to make a choice between obtaining a house or having a wedding with all the whistles and bells. One such couple that I worked with were planning a typical wedding with over 150 invited guests, but changed their agenda when the opportunity to obtain their own home fell into their laps as they started to plan for their wedding. After giving their situation much thought, they decided to cancel the large wedding and replace it with a very personal marriage ceremony with 10 invited family members and friends. A small, cozy inn was secured for both the ceremony and a wedding dinner for the intimate group of people. The newlyweds departed from the inn the following morning for a short honeymoon and issued wedding announcements to remaining family members and friends on their return. Several months later, they held an open house and reception party at their new home. Their wedding plan contained all the essentials but was focused in a way that allowed them to make that giant leap from apartment living to home ownership immediately upon becoming "Mr. and Mrs."

An intimate wedding also may be the best way to begin your new lives together if your family makes planning your wedding a nightmare. Why put yourselves through unnecessary irritation and expense if you know that your wedding plans will be impossible to accomplish because of family turmoil. There is no written law that states you must have a large wedding to enter into a rapturous and blissful state of married life. Couples that have a small, intimate wedding are just as married and have gotten there with much less expense and fuss. Your wedding plans and the wedding itself should be within your reach, whatever your financial resources are. If your wedding plans are causing you immeasurable difficulty and anxiety, on one or several different levels, perhaps the answer to your problem is to circumvent it all by having a beautiful, small, intimate wedding day.

❧ Call on a Posse of Elders to Help You

If you need help and ideas to keep your wedding within your financial means, get in touch with the American Association of Retired Persons (AARP) chapter or senior citizens' group in your area. You may find semi-retired professionals who can assist you with music, photography, food, and the like for your wedding plan. Many senior citizens are also capable of doing little jobs like creating personalized favors or wedding party gifts. Most retired people keep up their skills and love to have a project now and then to work on, and the extra income that goes with it. They will usually cost you less than someone that has to maintain a license and advertise his or her services. There is an army of retired professional people out there who can help you cut wedding costs.

❧ File Those Receipts and Notes

The last thing that is really important to any complicated plan that involves money is to be able to put your finger on your receipts and all the notes collected along the way. Keeping an accurate account of your expenses will help you maintain control of your wedding budget and adhere more firmly to your original plan. There are a number of efficient ways to accomplish this. You can create your own bridal log book that works very efficiently and is inexpensive. Here are two ideas that were used by prospective brides who were on a tight budget and realized the need to be very organized to accomplish this end.

One woman bought an accordion paper file folder from a local discount store. She labeled each pocket with all the various services and items needed for her wedding. Each time she collected information or paid a bill for that item, she placed the papers and receipts in the appropriate pocket of the file and, in addition, kept a log with a total of all expenses, showing expected costs, down payments, balances due, and a running total of funds left with which to work. Whenever she needed to attend to wedding business, she could literally go about with her entire wedding plan and budget under her arm, much like a purse. When a question came up about a particular part of her wedding plans, the information on that section was readily available because it was neatly filed away in the appropriate pocket and the expense log was always available. There are various sized folders on the market. Purchasing one with many pockets is a good idea for any size wedding plan. Also, using one with a tie-down cover prevents things from accidentally sliding out of the pockets. The folders cost about eight dollars and are available from most discount department stores, in their office supply section.

Janice and Randy, another couple planning a wedding on a tight budget, used the same idea, but instead of the accordion file folder, bought several pages with a pocket folder on the bottom of each. They placed a dozen or so pocket folder pages into a three ring notebook and labeled each pocket with the services they would be using. They then added several lined paper pages to the back of their "accounting" book for notes. Their guests lists, budget, and a running expense log was also kept in this notebook, along with all their payment receipts and written agreements, filed in the appropriate pocket.

These inexpensive ideas and wedding tools can be adapted to whatever your style may be. The important thing is to keep everything handy and organized for quick reference. Developing methods of staying organized will save you time, frustration, and money. It will also give you a sense of accomplishment and control as you proceed toward your big day.

Chapter Eight

Going to the Chapel: Church Weddings—Blending Old with New

✎ Creating A Personal Wedding Ceremony

If you are planning to be married in a religious ceremony, it is a very exciting time for marriage. Most religious groups today are encouraging and helping couples to incorporate personal selections of readings, prayers, and music into their marriage ceremony. A standard format is frequently used as a guideline that contains several choices or examples of Scripture and wording for each part of the service.

The wording that accompanies your exchange of rings and your marriage vows can be completely original if you so desire. In many cases, couples are writing their entire ceremony with the guidance and help of their pastor. In this way, the wedding ceremony is more individualized. The couple develops an ownership of their wedding ceremony because it is a true reflection of themselves. In addition, marriage is also a unification of families and members of each family have begun to increase their vocal and physical participation in the ceremony.

If you would like to take a more active part in creating your wedding ceremony you must first obtain guidelines from the particular denomination in which you choose to be married, or from the cleric that is going to facilitate your marriage. With a format in hand, you can then begin to select wording that fits you as a couple, and if you desire, bring members of your family, your attendants, and even your wedding guests into your marriage ceremony. Select music, prayers, and readings for the different passages, according to what sounds the most beautiful to you and what seems to best validate your identities and the family identities you bring to the marriage.

To get you started creating your own special ceremony, several examples of music, scripture, poetry, prayers, and wording for the ring service and vows are given on the following pages. For additional ideas on designing your own ceremony, or creating your own vows, consult the following sources: Janet Anastasio and Michelle Bevilaqua, *The Everything Wedding Book: Everything You Need to Know to Survive Your Wedding and Actually Enjoy It!* (Holbrook, Mass.: Bob Adams, Inc., 1993); Sharon C. Cook and Elizabeth Gale, *A Personal Wedding Planner* (Holbrook, Mass.: Bob Adams, Inc., 1992); and Barbara Eklof, *"With These Words . . . I Thee Wed" Contemporary Wedding Vows for Today's Couple* (Holbrook, Mass.: Bob Adams, Inc., 1989).

✎ Music

Music will be played during your ceremony at several points:

As Your Guests Are Being Seated

Romance	Sibelius
O Lovely Night (Barcarolle)	Offenbach
Perfect Happiness	Schuman
Duet	Mendelssohn
Romance Andante	Mozart
Madigan	Mozart
Church Sonata in C	Mozart
Air	from the "Water Music Suite" G. F. Handel
Jesu, Joy of Man's Desiring	J. S. Bach
Reverie	Debussy
Greensleeves	Anonymous

On a Lighter Note

Chapel of Love	Phil Spector, Ellie Greenwich, and Jeff Barry
Volare	Mitchell Parish and Domenico Modango
Camelot	Lerner and Loewe
Memories Are Made of This	Terry Gilkson, Richard Dehr, and Frank Miller
To the Aisle	Billy Dawn Smith and Stuart Wiener

As Your Wedding Party Starts Down the Aisle

Bridal Chorus	Wagner
Wedding Processional	Rodgers and Hammerstein
Joyful, Joyful, We Adore Thee	Beethoven

Vocal Music: Sung at Different Points During the Service

Follow Me	John Denver
All I Ask of You	Andrew Lloyd Webber
Sunrise, Sunset	Sheldon Harnick and Jerry Bock
My Prayer	George Boulanger and Jimmy Kennedy
We've Only Just Begun	Roger Nichols
Ave Maria	Franz Schubert, Op. 52
Hawaiian Wedding Song	Al Hoffman, Dick Manning
I Will Always Love You	Dolly Parton
Wind Beneath My Wings	Bette Midler
And I Love You So	Don McLean
The Rose	Amanda McBroom

Hymns: For the Entire Congregation to Sing

Day by Day	Stephen Schwarts
How Great Thou Art	Stuart K. Hine
You'll Never Walk Alone	Rodgers and Hammerstein
Amazing Grace	John Newton
I Asked The Lord	Johnny Lange and Jimmy Duncan
Love Lifted Me	Kenny Rogers

Recessional: At the End of the Ceremony

Ode To Joy	Beethoven
Bridal March	Mendelssohn
How Sweet It Is	James Taylor

To inquire about the different types of classical music that can be used for a wedding service, or to obtain a tape of the pieces you plan to use for your wedding ceremony, call National Public Radio at 1-800-75-MUSIC.

❧ Examples of Prayers, Poems, Readings and Vows

Opening Words (Clergy Speaks to Couple, Family, and Friends)

1. With deep affection for ———— and ———— we have gathered here today to witness and bless their mutual vows that will unite them in marriage. To this moment they bring the fullness of their hearts as a treasure to share with one another. They bring the dreams which bind them together. They bring that particular personality and spirit which is uniquely their own, and out of that will grow the reality of their life together. We rejoice with them at this outward symbol of an inward union of hearts and minds, and invite you to celebrate it in the presence of God.

(Source Unknown)

2. We gather together today to witness the commitment of ———— and ———— as they join in marriage. Marriage is not to be entered into lightly, but with commitment, mutual respect, and a sense of reverence. Love is one of the profoundest experiences that come to human kind. At its best it reduces our self-centeredness, deepens and enriches our personalities, and provides much of the meaning of life.

Two people in love do not live in isolation from the wider embraces of humanity. To achieve love is not to be absolved of social responsibility. For this reason, the institution of marriage is ordained as a public recognition of the private experience of love, and as a sanctifying of both parties to its greatest purpose.

Marriage symbolizes the ultimate intimacy between a man and a woman. Yet this closeness should not diminish but strengthen the individuality of each partner. Rilke once said that marriage is not a matter

> of creating a quick community of spirit by tearing down and destroying all boundaries, but rather a good marriage is that in which each appoints the other guardian of his [or her] solitude. . . . Once the realization is accepted that even between the closest human beings infinite distances continue to exist, a wonderful living side by side can grow up, if they succeed in loving the distance between them no less than they love their closeness.

So it is out of the resonance between individuality and union that love, whose incredible strength is equal only to its incredible fragility, is born and reborn. Today's celebration of human affection is therefore the outward sign of a sacred and inward commitment. Such a union can only be maintained by abiding will and faithfulness, and can be renewed by human response to the divine gift of love. In this spirit —— and —— stand before us and prepare to join their lives in love and loyalty.

(Adapted from a service by Arisian, pp. 106-7)

3. —— and —— have invited us here today to celebrate their love and commitment to each other. On their behalf, I welcome you to this service of worship. —— and ——, we are happy to be here to celebrate with you the love which has brought you together, and which has already given you such joy and meaning.

In an obvious, yet deeply profound and mysterious way, you bring together your own separate pasts, different in memories, traditions, hopes, and loves. That will not change, but it will color the future, so that even as you become one, you will always remain two.

Marriage is not intended to be a melting pot where differences cease to exist, but rather it is intended to be the relationship where you can be fully and honestly yourself, sharing at the deepest level all that life is and all that you are.

Today's celebration of human affection is an outward sign of an inward and sacred commitment. We rejoice with you as you stand before us and prepare to join your lives in love and loyalty.

(Adapted from services by Reverend John Westerhoff and Reverend Courtney Peterson)

4. We are assembled here in the presence of God to join this man and woman in holy marriage, which is instituted by God, regulated by God's commandments, blessed by our Lord Jesus Christ, and to be held in honor among us all.

Let us therefore reverently remember that God has established and sanctified marriage for the welfare and happiness of humankind. Our savior has declared that a man shall leave his father and mother and cleave to his wife.

He has instructed those who enter into this relationship to cherish a mutual esteem and love; to bear with each other's infirmities and weaknesses; to comfort each other in sickness, trouble, and sorrow; in honesty and industry to provide for each other and for their household; to pray for and encourage each other; and to live together as heirs of the grace of life. Into this holy estate these two persons come now to be joined.

(Adaptation from A Book of Worship for Free Churches, Source Unknown)

Prayers (Clergy)

1. Seldom, O Lord, have we had more cause to give thanks than we do now. For all good gifts come from you, and among them is the gift of love. We express to you our heartfelt joy and gratitude, praising you for all the persons who have brought us to this moment. We thank you especially for the rich heritage of love that surrounds ———— and ———— now, and that will encompass their lives in all the days to come. For grandparents, parents, brothers, sisters, we are grateful in special ways today, along with the countless gifts of love from so many others as well who have helped to shape their lives until now. Bless the love which ———— and ———— proclaim today, that the love which they have found together may deepen through all their days. Amen.

(Author Unknown)

2. Eternal God, you have given us the need to love and to be loved and the capacity for both. We pray that you will bless the love which ——— and ——— proclaim today, and that their love and care for each other may ever deepen. We pray that they may face life's cares and trials with hope and understanding; in their caring for one another; and that the life they live may be one of enduring love. Grant, we pray that their life may be a guide and inspiration to those around them, and be with them as they live together in this holy covenant, from this time forth and through all their days. Amen.

(Author Unknown)

Be thou magnified, O bridegroom, like Abraham, and blessed like Isaac, and increase like Jacob, walking in peace and living in righteousness...
And thou, O bride, be magnified like Sarah, and rejoice like Rebecca, and increase like Rachel, being glad in thy husband and keeping the bounds of the law...

Greek Orthodox Marriage Ceremony

Scripture (Clergy, Parents, Wedding Party)

Intreat me not to leave thee, or to return from following after thee: For whither thou goest I will go, And where thou lodgest, I will lodge. Thy people shall be my people, And thy God my God. Where thou diest, will I die, And there will I be buried. The Lord do so to me, and more also, If ought but death part thee and me.

Ruth I:16-17 (King James Version)

Then put on the garments that suit God's chosen people, his own, his beloved: compassion, kindness, humility, gentleness, patience. Be forbearing with one another, and forgiving, where any of you has cause for complaint; you must forgive as the Lord forgave you. To crown all, there must be love, to bind all together and complete the whole. Let Christ's peace be arbiter in your hearts; to this peace you were called as members of a single body. And be filled with gratitude. Let the message of Christ dwell among you in all its richness. Instruct and admonish each other with the utmost wisdom.

Colossians 3:12-17 (The New English Bible)

Readings (Maid of Honor/Best Man)

A good relationship has a pattern like a dance and is built on some of the same rules. The partners do not need to hold on tightly, because they move confidently in the same pattern, intricate but gay and swift and free, like a country dance of Mozart's. To touch heavily would be to arrest the pattern and freeze the movement, to check the endlessly changing beauty of its unfolding. There is no place here for the possessive clutch, the clinging arm, the heavy hand; only the barest touch in passing. Now arm in arm, now face to face, now back to back—it does not matter which. Because they know they are partners moving to the same rhythm, creating a pattern together, and being invisibly nourished by it.

The joy of such a pattern is not only the joy of creation or the joy of participation, it is also the joy of living in the moment. Lightness of touch and living in the moment are intertwined. One cannot dance well unless one is completely in time with the music, not leaning back to the last step or pressing forward to the next one, but poised directly on the present step as it comes. Perfect poise on the beat is what gives good dancing its sense of ease, of timelessness, of the eternal.

Anne Morrow Lindbergh

Every promise of the soul has innumerable fulfillments; each of its joys ripens into a new want. Nature, uncontainable, flowing, forelooking, in the first sentiment of kindness anticipates already a benevolence which shall lose all particular regards in its general light. The introduction to this felicity is in a private and tender relation of one to one, which is the enchantment of human life; which, like a certain divine rage, pledges him to the domestic and civic relations, carries him with new sympathy into nature, enhances the power of the senses, opens the imagination, adds to his character heroic and sacred attributes, establishes marriage, and gives permanence to human society.

Ralph Waldo Emerson essay on Love

A marriage makes of two fractional lives a whole. It gives to two purpose-less lives a work, and doubles the strength of each to perform it. It gives to two questioning natures a reason for living. It brings a new gladness to the sunshine, and new fragrance to the flowers, and new beauty to the earth, a new mystery to life."

Mark Twain

Children's Prayers (Couple's Children or the Flower Girl/Ring Bearer)

Father, we thank Thee for all things
For laughter and happiness this day brings,
For family and friends, love and care,
And all that makes the world so fair.

Help our family to do the things we should,
To be to others kind and good,
In all we do, in all we say,
To grow more loving every day. Amen.

Adapted from First Prayers and Graces

Thank you Lord
For this new family,
and all Thy gifts of love,
We give Thee thanks and praise.
Look down, O Father, from above,
And bless us all our days. Amen.

Adapted from First Prayers and Graces

Twinkle twinkle little star
Bless my new family, wherever you are.
Help us to be patient and kind each day
Let love be with us, at work and play.

Twinkle twinkle little star
Shine down upon us from afar.
Sprinkle stardust on the path to our door
And fill our home with sweet love evermore. Amen.

Adapted from Twinkle Twinkle Little Star

Poetry (Wedding Party)

Love one another, but make not a bond of love:
Let it rather be a moving sea between the shores of your souls.
Fill each other's cup but drink not from one cup.
Give one another of your bread but eat not from the same loaf.
Sing and dance together and be joyous, but let each one of you be alone,
Even as the strings of a lute are alone though they quiver with the same
music.
Give your hearts, but not into each other's keeping.
For only the hand of Life can contain your hearts.
And stand together yet not too near together:
For the pillars of the temple stand apart,
And the oak tree and the cypress grow not in each other's shadow.

Kahlil Gibran, The Prophet, pp. 15-16

Through the Year

God be with you in the Springtime
When the violets unfold,
And the buttercups and cowslips
Fill the fields with yellow gold;
In the time of apple blossoms,
When the happy bluebirds sing,
Filling all the world with gladness—
God be with you in the Spring!

God be with you in the Summer,
When the sweet June roses blow,
When the bobolinks are laughing
And the brooks with music flow;
When the fields are white with daisies
And the days are glad and long—
God be with you in the Summer,
Filling all your world with song.

God be with you in the Autumn,
When the birds and flowers have fled,
And along the woodland pathways
Leaves are falling, gold and red;
When the Summer lies behind you,
In the evening of the year—
God be with you in the Autumn,
Then to fill your heart with cheer.

God be with you in the Winter,
When the snow lies deep and white,
When the sleeping fields are silent
And the stars gleam cold and bright.
When the hand and heart are tired
With life's long and weary quest—
God be with you in the Winter,
Just to guide you into rest.

Jullian S. Cutler, in Felleman, pp. 38-39

Homily (Short Message Given by Clergy, Family, Wedding Party)

We live in a world where love is viewed as an impulsive or transient emotion. Love happens and love unhappens. Yet love is not simply a surge of emotion. Love is partly conscious decision. In the covenant of marriage, love and commitment become one and the same. Love nurtures commitment; commitment nurtures love. And in the exercising of love and commitment within marriage, a man and a woman find freedom for greater love and deeper commitment.

Reverend Dale R. Edwards

Questions to the Couple (Clergy)

1. ——— and ———, marriage is a lifetime commitment of love and sharing. Have you both considered as fully as possible the significance of your covenant with one another? "We Have."

2. Do you dedicate yourselves to the continuing task of building a deep and lasting love with each other? And do you dedicate yourselves to helping each other in all ways possible to live the most fully human life? Do you dedicate yourselves to helping each other meet the challenges of marriage with honest struggle, open words, and shared lives? And do you realize what you know to be love cannot be limited or contained, and must reach out beyond yourselves to your families and to the worlds in which your live? "We Do."

Reverend Worth Noyes

Promises (Bride and Groom)

In some ceremonies, it is customary for the couple to state promises to each other before the congregation, in addition to their wedding vows:

I love you ———, and I promise to be a loving and caring husband. I promise to always cherish your presence and place our marriage above all else.

I love you ———, and I promise to always be there for you. I promise to receive your love with love and to work hard at keeping our marriage true and everlasting.

Lighting of Unity Candle (Bride, Groom, Families)

Many ceremonies include the lighting of a central candle from two separate candles held by the bride and groom to symbolize the uniting of two lives into one. Family members can then light candles from the central flame to symbolize the uniting of families through the marriage of their children.

Support of Marriage (Clergy Asks of Families, Congregation)

Many women do not want to be "given away" and are using words that denote more of an understanding of support from family, friends, and community, such as this:

Who stands with this woman in marriage? The bride's parents and family answer the question with "we do." A short message of love to the bride and groom and his family can be given here.

Who stands with this man in marriage? The groom's parents and family answer the question with "we do." A short message of love to the groom and bride and her family can be given here.

Who stands with this couple in marriage? The congregation answers with "We all do" or "All their loving family and friends do." A short message of love given by one member of the congregation to the couple and both their families can be read here.

Prayers of Support (Clergy)

1. God of our mothers and of our fathers, hear our pledges encouraging and supporting this union of ——— and ———. Bless us as we offer our prayerful and loving support to their marriage. Bless them as they pledge their lives to each other. With faith in you and in each other, may this couple always bear witness to the reality of the love to which we witness this day. May their love continue to grow, and may it be a true reflection of your love for all. Amen.

Author unknown

2. Blessed God, creator of all life, look with favor upon this man and this woman who stand before you today to be joined in marriage. Give them wisdom and fortitude to navigate smoothly through life's bumpy roads together;

make each a source of encouragement and strength to one another in times of difficulty or sorrow. Let them be companions in happiness and sharers of each other's joy. Help them to be a good listener to one another and let their love grow and deepen as they experience the wonders and mysteries of life together. Enable them to recognize their faults and seek out each other's forgiveness with grace. Keep their marriage in perfect harmony with one another and the universe in which they dwell. Amen.

Author unknown

Marriage Vows (Clergy, Bride and Groom)

1. I ——, take you, —— to be my wife/husband. I offer my love. I offer my strength and support. I offer my faith and trust in you. I offer my friendship and laughter, so we may have a lifetime together filled with joy and understanding.

Adapted from vows by Rev. Courtney Peterson

2. In the sight of God's love and in the presence of our families and friends, I, ——, take you, ——, to be my wife/husband, promising to be a faithful and loving wife/husband and striving to grow with you in faith and understanding as long as we both shall live.

Source unknown

3. I, ——, in the name of God, take you, ——, to be my husband/wife, from this time onward, to join with you and to share with you all that is to come, to give and to receive, to speak and to listen, to inspire and to respond, and in all our life together to be loyal and to cherish you with my whole being, as long as we both shall live.

Source unknown

Ring's Symbolic Meaning (Clergy)

1. These rings are the symbol of the vows taken and the love affirmed. They are a circle of wholeness, the perfect form. These rings mark a commitment to a long journey together filled with wonder, surprises, laughter, tears, celebration, grief, and joy. May these rings glow in reflection of the warmth and the love that flows through you today.

Reverend Courtney Peterson

2. "The form of the ring being circular, that is round, and without end, means thus: that mutual love and hearty affection should roundly flow from

one to the other, as in a circle, that is continual and forever." (from a 17th century wedding ceremony)

Taken from The Customs of Mankind by Lillian Eichler, Garden City Pub., 1924

Exchange of Rings (Clergy, Bride, and Groom)

1. I give you this ring in love and with great joy, and as a pledge to honor you with my whole being.

Reverend Courtney Peterson

2. I give this ring as a symbol of my vow, and with all that I am and all that I have, I commit myself to you.

Reverend Courtney Peterson

3. I give you this sign of my love, knowing that love is precious and fragile, yet strong. I give you this sign of our love, an ever present symbol of the vows we have made here this day. I give you this ring as I give you my love.

Reverend Courtney Peterson

Ring Blessing (Clergy)

Bless these rings and make them a sacred reminder to this man and this woman of their holy marriage vows taken before their family and friends today. Let the endless circle of these rings be symbolic of their eternal love and union. Amen.

Reverend Courtney Peterson

Declaration of Marriage (Clergy)

———— and ————, having witnessed your vows for marriage before God and this congregation, I announce with great joy that you are from this time on, husband and wife.

Author unknown

Reading (Bride and Groom)

I am blessed above my kind, with another self—a life companion who is part of me—part of my heart and flesh and spirit—and not a fellow pilgrim who lags far behind, or flies ahead, or soars above me.

Side by side, my darling, we walk the ways of life; and the ray of light that falls upon the one illuminates the face of the other; the cloud that darkens the hope of one casts its sable shadow upon the other; and the storms that come will beat upon no single head but both will feel their might and brave their desolation.

Mark Twain (letter to his wife)

Closing Prayer (Clergy)

Bless them, O Lord our God, as Thou didst bless Zechariah and Elizabeth. Preserve them, O Lord our God, as Thou didst preserve Noah in the ark. Preserve them, O Lord our God, as Thou didst preserve Jonah in the belly of the whale. Preserve them, O Lord our God, as Thou didst preserve the three holy children from the fire, sending down upon them dew from heaven; and let that gladness come upon them which the blessed Helen had when she found the precious cross. Remember them, O Lord our God, as Thou didst remember Enoch, Shem, Elijah. Remember them, O Lord, our God, as Thou didst remember Thy forty holy martyrs, sending down upon them crowns from heaven. Remember them, O Lord our God, and the parents who have nurtured them, for the prayers of parents make firm the foundations of houses. Remember, O Lord our god, Thy servants, the groomsman and the bridesmaid of the bridal pair, who have come together in this joy.

Orthodox Marriage Service

Almighty God, by whose love the whole world is created, sustained, and redeemed, so fill ———— and ———— with the overflowing abundance of your grace that their lives may reflect your compassion for all. May their love for each other not blind them from the brokenness in the world. As you teach them to bind up each other's wounds, teach them also to heal the hurts of others. As their mutual respect orders their common life within the family, direct them to their share also in the shaping of a society in which human dignity may flourish and abound. At all times and in all seasons, may they rejoice to serve you and to give you thanks, through Jesus Christ our Lord. Amen.

Episcopal Marriage Service

Most gracious God, we give you thanks for your tender love in sending Jesus Christ to come among us, to be born of a human mother, and to make the way of the cross be the way of life. We thank you, also, for consecrating the union of man and woman in his Name. By the power of your Holy Spirit, pour out the abundance of your blessing upon this man and this woman. Defend them from every enemy. Lead them into all peace. Let their love for each other be a seal upon their hearts, a mantle about their shoulders, and a crown upon their foreheads. Bless them in their work and in their companionship; in their sleeping and in their waking; in their joys and in their sorrows; in their life and in their death. Finally, in your mercy, bring them to that table where your saints feast forever in your heavenly home; through Jesus Christ our Lord, who with you and the Holy Spirit lives and reigns, one God, for ever and ever. Amen.

or

O God, you have so consecrated the covenant of marriage that in it is represented the spiritual unity between Christ and his Church: Send therefore your blessing upon these your servants, that they may also love, honor, and cherish each other in faithfulness and patience, in wisdom and true godliness, that their home may be a haven of blessing and peace; through Jesus Christ our Lord, who lives and reigns with you and the Holy Spirit, one God, now and for ever. Amen.

The Blessing of the Marriage,
from The Book of Common Prayer (of the Episcopal Church), pp. 430-31.

Benediction (Clergy, Parents,)

Lord,
May they both praise you when they are happy
and turn to you in their sorrows.
May they be glad that you help them in their work
and know that you are with them in their need.
May they pray to you in the community of the Church,
and be your witnesses in the world.
May they reach old age in the company of their friends,
and come at last to the kingdom of heaven.
We ask this through Christ our Lord. Amen.

Catholic Marriage Blessing

May the Lord bless you and keep you. May the Lord make the light of his presence to shine upon you and be gracious unto you. May the Lord lift up His presence to you and grant you long life and health, the privilege of service together in every high and sacred cause; acknowledgment of life's deepest meanings; a deepening and growing love of one another; a life of peace in a world dwelling at peace. Amen.

Jewish Ancestral Blessing

Now you will feel no rain,
for each of you will be shelter to the other.
Now you will feel no cold,
for each of you will be warmth to the other.
Now there is no more loneliness,
for each of you will be companion to the other.
Now you are two bodies,
but there is only one life before you.
Go now to your dwelling place,
to enter into the days of your togetherness,
And may your days be good and long upon the earth.

Apache Marriage Blessing

Introduction of Married Couple (Clergy)

With great pleasure, I present to you ———— and ————, husband and wife, wife and husband.

❧ Things to Remember

If you plan to have your clergy perform your marriage service in a state other than that in which his or her church is located, be sure to check with that state's secretary of state. In some cases, a clergy coming from another state to perform a marriage service must obtain permission from a legal authority in that state to legally perform the ceremony. Failure to do so could nullify the marriage.

Schedule adequate time together to select music, readings, scripture, poetry, and the like for your wedding service, and stay focused on this project until it is finished to your liking. Inform your family and wedding party early on if you want them to take an active part in your ceremony, so they can prepare for it. If a particular family member or close friend cannot attend your marriage ceremony, ask him or her to write something that can be read aloud by one of your attendants during the service, so that he or she will be there with you in spirit. If you desire active participation from your congregation, make the response wording available to them in large, bold print. Place a copy of the original finished draft of your marriage ceremony with your wedding keepsakes. On each wedding anniversary, select a passage from your ceremony to read aloud to each other. Make your "anniversary reading" a family event so your children can witness and hear how their family began.

Chapter Nine

"Let's Celebrate!"

Reception Recipes for Inclusion, Fun, and Excitement

It's a new era in wedding receptions. Relax and enjoy is the password. The identical pattern of yesterday's receptions is changing. Celebration is the new word being used to describe the type of party couples are planning to follow their marriage ceremony. Instead of letting their special day slip by in a stressful blur of things that have to be done, they too want to have a great day with lots of fun and memories. Some brides and grooms are going out of their way to insure that their celebration party will be a really enjoyable time for all.

One couple, whose ceremony took place at a beautiful lakefront property, sent a note with their invitation, inviting their guests to bring their swim suits if the weather was hot.

> We were married in the middle of July and knew that we could have a very hot day for our wedding. We wanted everyone to relax and enjoy the day and each other's company and just have fun. It seemed natural to invite our family and friends to come prepared to have a swim if they wanted to. Most everyone took us up on this offer as our wedding day temperatures reached into the nineties. Not too long after the food had been served, many guests changed into their swim suits and dove into the lake for a refreshing swim. We even had several boats decorated with flowers and balloons and many of us took a spin around the lake honking the horns, all dressed in our wedding clothes.

A couple being married for the second time held their wedding reception at the home of the bride's parents. They hired a catering company to serve their guests a delicious menu of steak, lobster, and salads, served under a colorful tent. The tables were decorated with white linen table cloths, rainbow-colored napkins, and home-grown floral center pieces, each tied with a pink and green balloon. Their celebration had a party look and feel to it from the moment their guests started to arrive. The marriage took place in front of a lilac bush in full bloom. The formal ritual of a receiving line was passed up in favor of a general mingling of guests. Music floated over the air from a collection of CDs. Their reception was more of an informal social gathering and reacquainting of old friends and family members.

> We had not seen many of our family and guests for a period of time so we wanted a party for them and ourselves with a relaxed atmosphere, good food, and lots of time for catch-up conversations. We cut our wedding cake in the usual manner after the meal, which added just a little touch of tradition to our celebration. The cake however was not traditional. It was a simple shortcake, frosted with tons of whipped cream and a bride and groom cake top of course. A large crystal bowl of strawberries was set off to the side of the cake so that our guests could make themselves an old fashioned strawberry short cake dessert.

Tim and Robin, who had moved away from their original homes in the east to a far western state, planned a white water raft ride on the day following their formal ceremony and reception, for family and friends who wanted this experience. "A lot of our guests were coming from afar to attend our wedding and we wanted them to have fun doing something very informal and different. We simply extended our wedding day party into the next day with our invitation to ride the rapids. We also thought that the raft ride would be an unforgettable experience for all of us to do together and it really was."

Creating a celebration that is not just another wedding reception may be something that you have given some thought to. Think about how you can use new and different ideas by themselves or in combination with the standard reception program to personalize your reception and give it a true party-like atmosphere.

✎ "Do We Really Need a Head Table?"

Some couples are electing not to have a head table per se, but to seat themselves with special family members or friends in the center of the eating area. The remaining people in their wedding party and family are then seated in a scattered fashion at the tables of the other guests. In this way, the attendants and family members are set out among the guests to set the tone of the celebration party. They can relate information and stories about the couple and all the wedding preparations, which is usually of interest to the other guests, and makes good mealtime conversation. This also gives the party a less rigid atmosphere when the bride and groom are seated in the center of the activity rather than on the periphery of it all.

Not having to have a head table may also let you consider places for your reception that you had previously thought were not roomy enough, because of the head table factor. Being seated at a place of honor among your family and friends may seem more natural and help you both to better enjoy and remember your first meal as a married couple.

◈ Win/Win Seating for Your Guests

How your guests are seated at your reception party is a personal choice. If you are going to have a formal dinner, it is usually the rule to set out place cards at each table with the various guests' names on them. Some couples simply sit relatives together and friends together at alternate tables. Arranging who is to sit next to whom takes some time and a little bit of consideration. If this becomes too complicated, some couples do not attempt to assign seating for the reception meal but simply let their guests seat themselves.

If you are going to designate where your guests are going to sit, you should think about personalities and try not only to sit certain groups of people together but also sprinkle those people around who always seem to liven up a party. If you try to seat the more lively or animated couples or individuals together with those that seem more sedate, your seating arrangement will have a more festive balance to it. Many times this can help to add a pleasant atmosphere and tone to your dinner reception.

The types of tables you choose for a formal sit down dinner or a buffet are important to comfortable seating of your guests. Round tables always allow a more blended conversation among your guests and have a warmer, cozier look than the long rectangular type. A floral centerpiece on a round table gives each seated guest a decorated space at your party. If you do not have a choice of round tables and must go with the rectangular ones, request that they be arranged to seat no more than six in each group. In this way, everyone seated at a particular table can hear what each other is talking about and feel more a part of the group's conversation. Your invited guests will enjoy your wedding feast even more if they feel comfortably seated and able to easily converse with others at their table.

☙ Raising the Roof with Music and Laughter

Newlyweds want their families and guests to have a great time celebrating at their wedding. That's one of the reasons that you hired someone to provide music, for entertainment and dancing. One mistake that seems to occur at many wedding receptions is having music that is too loud. Most people don't appreciate loud music because it is impossible to talk to one another when you cannot hear what the other person is saying.

Disc jockeys, especially, seem to feel that if the volume is turned up high, people will get out onto the dance floor and have a good time. Of course this is not true. Some of your guests will not like to dance, and the ones that do will probably not want to dance every dance. Some will just like to enjoy sitting or wandering about, talking and watching the others out on the dance floor. So instruct your master of ceremonies (MC) to keep the music at a level that permits dancing and conversation at the same time. Your guests will stay longer, mingle better, and enjoy the music and dancing more with this win/win combination.

Having music and dancing that everyone can join in with, even if they can't dance or sing, makes a true party atmosphere. Everyone likes to do line dances, circle dances, and other "good time dances" at weddings because perfect steps are not required. Make up some leg ribbons with small bells attached and have a "ring the wedding bells" dance by having everyone tie one to his or her ankle or wrist for a lively line or circle celebration dance.

A great way to get all your guests into the music is to have one or several sing alongside. Your MC, or someone with a good musical voice, can get this going. Have printed copies of the lyrics to the songs that you want to do on each of your tables. Use colored paper for their printing and tie a contrasting colored ribbon at the corner. Set one of your sing-along programs at each guest setting so that it is available for use when the time is ready for this part of your party.

"Love and Marriage" is a good sing along. It can be done in a "round," by splitting your reception guests into three groups. It's an easy thing to have the MC do and sets a fun tone to your wedding celebration. Songs that can be done with an echo on the part of some of your guests are also fun. Millions of people used to enjoy singing along and acting as the echo of Eddie Cantor as he sang his famous rendition of "Making Whoopee"! It's a fun song to sing in echo fashion at wedding celebration parties.

If you make the words available, your guests will sing to you and love doing it. This activity provides a musical experience for those guests that don't want to or perhaps can't get up and dance at your wedding. Use your imagination and search out love songs that are fun to sing in several ways and have your MC scatter them throughout the dancing music.

✈ Wedding Cakes that Tell Who You Are

The wedding cake had its origins as a symbol of fertility. Today, the wedding cake is thought of as a symbol of celebration and unity. Couples are also using the wedding cake to tell or remind their guests something about themselves. Different shapes, flavors, and frosting are now being used to add personal touches to the once traditional wedding cake.

People that love boating may want to have a wedding cake that replicates their boat, using a basic boat design and illustrating all the tiny details on their boat with decorative frosting. A couple that just purchased a new home may want to replicate it in the design of their wedding cake. Little fancy touches such as their new married names can be placed on the door or lamp post. Couples that are involved in genealogy may want to have a cake in the shape of a family tree, decorating the different limbs of the tree cake with family names and other items of interest about their heritage. The lace pattern on the bridal gown can be repeated on the frosting of the cake to tie it into the dress.

Cake tops have expanded from the standard bride and groom figures to different types of brides and grooms atop the cake. The figurine's skin and hair color can be purchased to mimic the actual couple. The cake top bride and groom may be dressed to fit the theme of their wedding such as a western look. There are now several cake tops with a country type bride and a cowboy, complete with horse shoes, boots and lariat. A skilled artisan can make up or adapt any dress for cake top figurine.

If you cannot find the cake top that produces the desired effect you are searching for, you can make or have your cake top made to order, using ceramic reproduction. One mother, enrolled in a ceramic class for diversional activity, created a cake top, table decorations, and favors for her daughter's spring wedding. The cake top was custom painted to resemble the coloring of the couple and some of the details of their wedding attire. Each item that she turned out had the additional quality of being personalized with the couple's initials, and wedding date etched into the bottom. Ceramics classes are taught in most areas and usually someone is available for hire to make items if you do not have the available time for this project.

There are many pieces of wedding theme greenware available for purchase. Greenware is unbaked clay, predesigned into figurines, that the student buys and decorates by painting them with a particular color scheme. After the pieces are painted, they are baked to a hardened finish. Floral centerpiece holders for tables, candlestick holders, and favors, all with a wedding motif, are a few of the items that can be found in ceramic greenware for use at your wedding reception.

Another possible way to obtain an unusual cake top, is to employ a glass-maker to design and make one to your specifications. Glassblowing is an old art and glassblowers can usually be located through state-organized craft groups. Glassblowers sometimes also put on exhibitions of their skills in blowing and shaping glass figurines at local and state-run country fairs.

↝ Remember Your Vegetarian and Non-Sugar-Eating Guests

Regardless of the type of meal you are planning for your wedding reception, it is smart to take into consideration the eating habits of all the guests at your reception. There are sure to be some that are non-meat eaters, or for health reasons, can't eat sugar. It is a thoughtful gesture to have a special entree available for your vegetarian guests, in addition to whatever else is set for the main course. An ample supply of different types of fruit should always be available. It will not only provide a wider selection of food for the invited guests that choose to avoid sugar or animal fat, but also make your meal more colorful.

Most caterers are sensitive to the different types of dietary habits and should be able to assist you with appropriate food suggestions. You can also look up different recipes in a vegetarian cookbook to get a sense of what would appeal to this group of eaters. (Vegetarian lasagna is wonderful!) The important thing is to recognize the different eating habits of your invited guests, and have something delicious prepared for all of them.

↝ For the Birds

Rice, a symbol of fertility, has long been used by family and guests to shower the married couple as they leave the church or set out from the reception for their honeymoon trip. Because rice is dangerous for birds to consume, it is no longer commonly used. Instead, bird seed is being thrown. It is sold in some places in little packets and called "love seed." A wonderful and fun way of making bird seed or "love seed" available for your guests to throw at your wedding or reception is to make cloth roses and fill each of them with a little seed. They add to the decorations at your wedding scene and are easy to make or have made. They also make a nice favor for your guests to take home, to be set into a bud vase and used as a small room accent.

The stem of the rose is made using a six-inch pipe cleaner or a small wooden dowel. The rose is made of colored satin, taffeta, velvet, or other types of material. Cut the material into four- or five-inch squares and machine sew up the edges of one side of each square. Insert a pipe cleaner or dowel into one of the open ends of the square and wrap the base of the material and pipe cleaner together using a green floral tape. Wrap the length of the pipe cleaner or dowel with the floral tape. Twisting the material a little as you begin to wrap it will give the flower a few little gathers that make it resemble a budded rose.

Fill the "rose" with bird seed and turn the rough edges into the flower to hold the seed inside. Tie a card with your married names and wedding date to the rose base with a satin ribbon and have one of your ushers hand them out to your guests as they enter the place of the marriage ceremony. If you are not allowed to throw anything at the place of your marriage ceremony, place the "roses" together in a vase on a table at your celebration banquet or set one at each place setting for your guest. They can than shower you with "love seeds" as you leave the reception at the end of the party.

The few supplies that you will need to make your roses are available at a crafts store or crafts section of a discount store. Many times, you can match your roses to your bridesmaids' dresses by ordering a yard or two of the same material when the dresses are ordered. To figure out how much material to order, simply take the square inch dimensions of the size flower you want to make and multiply this by the number of flowers you will need. Divide this number into the size of the material available and you will come up with the approximate yardage needed to do the job. For example: To make a rose that is about 2 inches when finished will require a piece of material that is 3" by 3", or 9 square inches. If you want 100 roses, you will need 900 square inches of material. Divide this number into the total square inches of your material to get the amount of material needed to make your 100 roses. (One yard, or 36" of material that is 36" wide, is equal to 1296 square inches. 1296 divided by 900 = .7 yards of material to do the job.)

Be sure to keep several roses for yourselves and your parents. The small satin roses make a nice keepsake and reminder of your special day. They look pretty when set into a bud vase and displayed alongside your wedding glasses or pictures.

⋆ The Scent of a Flower

There was a time when the floral arrangements for weddings not only looked beautiful but also smelled wonderful. Both the senses of sight and smell were peaked by the lovely arrangements held and worn by the wedding party and used to decorate the church and reception site. Today the flowers at weddings are still very beautiful but the scent has disappeared from many. Local florists that I spoke with said that it is due to various strains being hybridized and or forced to grow too rapidly. Florists have access to larger selections of blooms with more colors to choose from now, but sadly, the scent has been bred out of many. The end result is floral arrangements that look very pretty but are missing the wonderful perfumes.

There are still a few old standbys that have not been robbed of their scents such as Stephanotis and Gardenias. These are flowers that were once widely used in wedding bouquets and mothers' corsages. There are also a few types of roses that still have a wonderful smell. They are the lavender Lavande Rose (pronounced "la-vaun"), the Royalty Red Rose, the McGredy Ivory Rose, and the deep yellow Victory Rose.

Ask your florist to use flowers that have a scent to make up your floral arrangements. Long after your wedding day has passed, you and others will recall memories of it, whenever you encounter the scent of your wedding flowers. You may have to speak with your florist several months ahead of time to have him or her locate and acquire beautifully scented blooms for your wedding arrangements.

Besides hothouse flowers, there are other flowers that have pretty scents and can be grown in common flower gardens and used in your wedding scheme. Depending on your wedding date, some of these can be gathered and used in addition to those of the professional's floral arrangements, to decorate and perfume your wedding ceremony and reception party. Mother Orchids have an intoxicating smell to them. Sweet Williams, found in many flower gardens, have a wonderful spicy scent. Plumeria, a fragrant and sweet smelling houseplant with pretty red-orange flowers, can be grown and used to decorate your reception site. Plumeria is a flower frequently found in

Hawaiian leis because of their color and scent. Lavender flowers and foliage add additional fragrance to wedding bouquets. Apple blossoms can be used to decorate and add pretty aromas to your reception hall. Jasmine is another often overlooked flower that can add sweet smelling memories to wedding days. Don't just concentrate on the color of your flowers for your wedding arrangements. Think also about selecting ones that offer added stimulant and sensual effect derived from a beautiful scent. Both you and guests will notice the difference. It will feel and smell more like your wedding took place in an enchanted garden, where ever it is held.

✎ *Wedding Favors*

The dictionary describes a favor as "something given as a token of love, affection, or remembrance. A small decorative gift." Favors have long been part of the wedding ceremony, and at one time in history, were actually hung on the wedding cake to be handed out to those present following the marriage ceremony. Today, favors are usually set out at each place setting or piled onto a table in some fashion at the reception party. Favors are fun to make and can come in many forms and shapes.

One very easy and pretty favor can be made up of a small circle or square of netting material that encloses candy or nuts and is then wrapped with a pretty ribbon with your names and wedding date fixed to the favor. You can elect to cut your own circles or squares from several yards of netting secured at a fabric shop, or purchase them in packets of precut material. Hortense Hewett, a large company located in Rexburg, Idaho, is one of several wedding accessory businesses that sells precut netting for wedding favors (phone: 1-800-821-2504).

Chocolate kisses or candy coated almonds are frequently used to fill favors of this kind. The Hershey Company, located in Hershey, Pennsylvania, will supply you with kisses by the pound, in the standard silver foil or various pastel colored foil. You can get about one pound, or one hundred kisses, for $3.10. (Call 1-800- 233-2168 for details.) These kinds of favors can also be mixed with sweet-smelling potpourri. You can use herbs mixed with your own dried flower petals to add a touch of symbolism to your favors. The herb's symbolic meaning can be included with your names and wedding date on the little card attached to the favor.

Bookmarks make wonderful, small decorative gifts to use as wedding favors. Some invitation companies offer several types of bookmarks that allow you to include your vows or special thank you message on them. You can also explore the possibility of having your engagement picture used to make your bookmarks, through some invitation companies, a local print shop, or your photographer. One couple, both recovering alcoholics, used the Alcoholics Anonymous prayer on one side of their bookmarks, and a personal thank you poem on the reverse side, with their names and the wedding date signed at the bottom. Bookmarks of this kind are very personal, meaningful, and almost always kept and used by wedding guests. Coronet Thermographers, located in Providence, Rhode Island, has a nice assortment of bookmark favors and are wonderful to work with (phone: 1-401-944-7100).

Brichcraft Thermographers, located in Boston, Massachusetts, has a great idea for a wedding favor. It is a small box that serves as a place card and favor at your reception. Your names and date are printed on the front in various color foils. There is also a space to insert the table number and the name of your guest. You then can fill the little box with different types of candy. With one purchase, you can provide organized seating at your reception dinner and a small remembrance of your wedding day for your guests. For information, call 1-617-878-5152.

✒ "Insteadofs"

Many couples are doing wonderful and different things at their weddings today to give a deeper meaning to the event. One of the things that is being done to add remembrance to the day is the releasing of a pair of doves by the bride and groom. This act is starting to replace the traditional throwing of the wedding bouquet and garter. Perhaps it is becoming popular because it can be done jointly by the bride and groom, and is symbolic of their new life together.

Instead of throwing the wedding bouquet and garter, stand together on a table above your dancing guests and strew sweet smelling potpourri and good luck herbs over your family and friends as they dance by.

Instead of throwing the bouquet and garter, have a balloon dance to pass on some marriage magic. Stand together in the center of the dance floor and give a ribbon tied balloon to each person that dances next to you until all of your colorful balloons are dispersed.

Instead of throwing your bouquet, give it to a very special friend.

Instead of walking down the aisle to meet your groom in the front of the church or marriage site, enter from opposite directions and come together simultaneously to begin your marriage ceremony. Instead of the bride's walking down the aisle on the arm of her father, walk down the aisle together, bride and groom, arm and arm, to your marriage site.

Instead of toasting with wine, have your wedding toast done using water, to celebrate and pay reverence to the wonder of all life on planet earth.

When you begin to plan your wedding reception, think of things that are symbolic, meaningful, and fun to do. Your celebration party will be more enjoyable for you and your invited guests, and you will gain joyful memories of a time when your family and friends gathered to witness your marriage and to celebrate!

Chapter Ten

Memorable Toasts to Each Other

Preserving the Moment Forever

Marriage is a profound act. A few well-chosen words of love and support, given to each other at the onset of marriage, will help you always to remember the moment that it all began. It doesn't take a poet laureate to create words of deep meaning and love to mark this wondrous new beginning, only the ability to say what you feel in your heart—words that capture the essence of your true feelings and will echo your commitment and love for each other as the years pass.

A toast to each other can be done at your reception, or during the privacy of a special honeymoon moment. Write out a wedding toast to your bride or groom and place it under your life-mate's plate when you are out to dinner some night, as a loving surprise for him or her. To continue the romance, create a new toast each year and deliver it to one another on your anniversary. As the years pass, you will acquire a very personal and special collection of personal prose and poetry. A wonderful way to preserve your original toasts to each other is to have them reproduced in calligraphy and then encased in a beautiful frame for additional wedding remembrance.

The following are some examples of toasts that can be used or easily adapted with your own intimate and special words that ring true to your feelings about your love for one another.

To ———,
May we experience each day with love and joy in our hearts and may our marriage continue to grow ever deeper and stronger through the years to come. As the days turn into weeks and the weeks into months and then into

years, may we never forget our joyous beginning and our love and commitment to each other that we enter into this day.

To my lovely wife ————. All that I ever dreamed of, all that I can ever hope for has been granted to me this day. I will cherish you for all eternity.

To my wonderful husband ————, kind and gentle and giving. The heavens have led me to you. I will honor you and grow old with you. I will love you for all eternity.

To ————, the joy of my life, the love of my heart, the essence of my being. My world is wondrous because of you.

To ————, ever caring, ever loving. The Great Spirit has rained joy down upon us this day. I will cherish you forever.

To ————. Today we begin our lives together as one. May all our tomorrows be a reflection of this hour, this day. I love you sincerely, your husband ————.

To ————. Today we celebrate our new beginning as man and wife. May we savor the passing days as they turn into years. May all our tomorrows be built with trust, love, and joy.

May we always share each other's sunshine. May our rains always be gentle. May our sweet music of love be endless.

May we always find each other irresistible and take the time to help our love grow ever greater. May we never forget the star-spangled nights and the sunny days filled with the sparkle of love. May we live our lives out to the fullest, always surrounding each other with joyful and happy hearts.

May our joyous love always give us hope, courage, and great heart to face the future together and cherish each day spent as husband and wife.

To ————. May the glow of this magic day always light up our path. May the hustle and bustle of daily living never dampen our spirit of love for each other.

To my wonderful wife ————. To her kind and gentle ways. To a lifetime of love and happiness together.

To my sweet husband ———. Never more than a heartbeat away, drifting in and out of my thoughts at work and play. To a lifetime of great happiness together.

To my beautiful wife/husband. Today you have made my life complete. To our marriage and a lifetime of fun, love, and happiness.

To ———. You are the light of my life. You are the music within my heart. May all our years to come be bound with endless love.

To ———. Because of that certain look, that certain smile, my eyes caught yours and a new life began with blue skies and sunny days. May the joy of this moment be with us always.

Let us always remember the joy of this day, as we enjoy the passing years together. May we always continue to grow in love and spirit and partake of life to its fullest.

May we always remember this wonderful day as we start our life together. May we always be able to turn back the hands of time as the years roll by and rekindle love's flame.

May we always walk in sunshine. May good fortune always be with us. May our cup always be filled. May the birds always sing our song. May the music never cease.

May our love always be a reflection of nature's beautiful seasons, the warmth of a summer day, the richness of autumn, the coziness of winter, the promise of spring. I deeply love you ———.

To my darling wife/husband ———. I will never forget this day and the happiness and magic we felt as we took our sacred marriage vows. I will always love you and cherish this wondrous gift of your love.

To life and to our love, to each new day we will share together, may our marriage be long and filled with love, happiness, support, and kindness toward each other.

May our prevailing winds always be fair. May our share of sunshine be plentiful. May our ancestors watch over our paths and guide us into safe harbors, to a long and wonderful life together.

To my wonderful wife/husband. To a life filled with joy and bliss. To many years of committed love. To a home filled with happy people. May our union be loving, long, and filled with cheer. Let us never forget that in each other we have found love, a wondrous treasure.

Chapter Eleven

Ethnic Themes

Telling It Like It Is

The dictionary defines "ethnic" as a special status of a social group based on complex and variable traits, including religious, linguistic, ancestral, and physical characteristics. Where once we tried to hide cultural differences to blend in, today celebrating our differences is becoming the norm. Wedding celebrations, in particular, seem to be the perfect place to acknowledge and appreciate the ancestry of two different individuals and families whose lives are about to merge.

Ethnic traditions give a special status to a particular group of people. Many beautiful and meaningful traditions can be taken from your ethos and brought into your wedding ceremony and reception by exploring your family tree and the varied cultures that may share its branches.

> More than one ancestor is struggling within you! We are all of mixed blood—very mixed, indeed, but more good than bad. You have two parents, four grandparents, eight great grandparents, sixteen great-great grandparents, thirty-two great-great-great-grandparents, and so on! Go back only ten generations, and you accumulate 2,046 ancestors on the way. You are descended from possibly 1,024 different people of the generation that saw the Mayflower cross the ocean. There is nothing so democratic as a family tree, if you climb into all its branches!
>
> *Albert W. Palmer*
> *Our American Heritage by Charles L. Wallis, Harper & Row, 1970*

More and more couples are desiring to do just this and are lending focus to their cultural heritage by bringing some or all of the color of their particular past and destiny into their wedding scene. It can add pageantry, deep meaning, and remembrance to your marriage ceremony and the celebration party that follows.

The special status of each of your ancestral social groups can be emphasized in many ways. Great or moderate focus can be placed on the characteristics of the particular people from which each of you has descended. So follow some of the footprints and paths of your ancestors. Let their presence be known and felt throughout your day. Their blessings will fall upon your marriage as the color and beauty of your roots is heard, seen, understood, and passed on to future generations. This is perhaps one of the greatest wedding gifts you can share with each other, your families, and your friends.

You can add a little ethnic flavor to your wedding day by incorporating one or more items that denote something about your rich cultural past. This can be done through flowers, words, music, poetry, or dress. During your reception party, you can continue to impart color from your past through these avenues and also include some ethnic foods and dance if you desire.

It would be impossible to examine in any depth the ethnicity of all groups of people in this short book. Instead, I will focus on some stories, customs, and traits of several countries and cultures to set the course. You, the reader, can take it from there to add personal ethnic details to your wedding day celebration by giving focus to your particular cultural heritage.

❧ African-American Ceremonies

Tammey D. Pettyjohn, a chemical engineer at Tuskegee University, and Clay La-Morris Jones, a general contractor from Americus, Georgia, knew when they started to plan for their wedding day that their ethnicity would play a very important role. "We started out by having our invitations hand painted to depict a silhouette bust of the heads of a black woman and man, with colorful African, Kente cloth, head dress. The invitation spoke well of what was to come at our marriage and reception celebration."

Because there were many family members, the wedding party had 12 bridesmaids, 12 groomsmen, 4 junior bridesmaids, 3 junior groomsmen, a bell ringer, "and a beautiful set of twin flower girls!" The guest list included over six hundred family, relatives, friends, and coworkers!

> I had two seamstresses from Nigeria and Ghana help me design and construct traditional-looking African dress for all of our immediate family and attendants. The bridesmaids were dressed in strapless dresses with a long scarf draped around their necks and a Neferetti headpiece to match their

dresses. The maid of honor was dressed identically but her headpiece was done in all black material. The junior bridesmaids' dresses were similar and had a very African, exotic look to them, by designing the bodice with just one long sleeve. Their African headpieces were also slightly different from the bridesmaids. These young girls wore Nigerian wrap dresses with a headdress to match. The twin flowergirls, also dressed in Kente cloth designs, tossed colorful potpourri on the red carpet as they preceded me down the aisle.

All the outfits were made out of, or incorporated in some way, Kente cloth, designed by the Ashanti people of Ghana, West Africa. "The striking designs in the cloth are symbols of a diverse African people and our struggle for equality. The colors are symbolic: red for blood that was shed by our slave ancestors, black for our people, green for the vegetation of Africa, and gold for its mineral wealth."

The men in the bridal party dressed in traditional black tuxedos with bright red-, green- and black-colored Kente cloth hats, crisscross ties, and chest banners. There were also twelve "hostesses," all dressed in shiny black dresses, with a touch of Kente cloth across their sleeves and a Kente cloth headpiece to match. "Their job was to keep things organized and flowing since we had so many guests respond to our wedding invitation!" The groom was dressed in an ivory tuxedo with a metallic gold turban-like hat, chest banner, and a crisscross tie held in place by a small jeweled medallion. "The medallion was adapted from a piece of woman's jewelry to add a regal touch to his outfit." His bride wore a straight, fitted, ivory colored, European-design wedding dress. Her headpiece was specially styled to give the image of an African regal headwrap with a short veil, made of lace and attached to one side of the head dress. A red carpet and several ivory colored plant stands holding large ferns were stationed at intervals down the aisle to set a very royal scene for the couple and all their attendants.

One small child acted as a "bell ringer" and preceded the bride down the aisle. The bride, a music minor in college, chose unconventional music with which to walk down the aisle. "The Wedding Song," by Kenny G., was played by a single flutist. The bride carried a bouquet of silk, wild African flowers of red, gold, black, and grey. "My bouquet looked very exotic and was arranged so that I could split it in two when I reached the altar and our families. Before I took my place with my groom, I gave each of our mothers half of my bouquet and kissed them, and then we all paid tribute, through verse, to our ancestors and the foundation they had created for us. This is an old ritual in Africa and is called Libation."

Our wedding ceremony incorporated original marriage vows that made mention again of our ancestors. A family circle was formed and each family member took part in some aspect of our ceremony. A member of each of our families welcomed both Clay and myself into our new families and there was a candle lighting ceremony for our mothers, using two white candles and one red one. Red is also a symbol of fidelity and purity in the African nation. At one special point in the ceremony, a prayer was offered up for my deceased father.

Five pieces of gospel music were sung and played on the organ and flute during the ceremony. One of the pieces they chose was "I.O.U. Me" by B. B. and C. C. Winans.

The ritual of Jumping the Broom was incorporated into the last part of the ceremony, just before the couple were pronounced man and wife by their minister. He read these solemn words to them:

"In America, customs among people of color had to be recreated. When West Africans were brought to these shores some 400 years ago, they were stripped of their culture. These enslaved people of color were spiritual people, so they had to become creative with respect to rituals they had lost. Out of this creativity came Jumping the Broom. Jumping the Broom symbolizes jumping from the old life as two into the new life as one with God as your guide.

After the wedding, while the married couple and their families were with their photographer, their guests were entertained with champagne and a showing of African art put on display at the entrance to the reception hall.

When it was time for the guests to be seated, a wonderful musician played music on a set of African drums so the hostesses knew it was time to open the doors to the reception hall. We came into the hall after our guests were seated and walked under an arch of eight large colorful feathers being held for us by several of our attendants, and down a red carpet to two large decorated wicker chairs, set up on a platform. A female dance-artist performed an African dance for us and our guests after we were seated. We then received each guests in turn as they walked up the red carpet to greet us. Our gift table was set to one side to receive and display our treasures so generously bestowed upon us by family and friends.

Tammey reports that their wedding took eight months to organize and put together.

I had to really search for African ideas, customs, and traditions for our wedding and this took some time to do. I used a royal theme to give a little focus to past kings and queens of various African tribes and adapted simple clothing patterns and bright colors throughout our wedding to capture our

African ethnicity. Everything went off well, and because of the many ethnic ideas we incorporated into it, the day was very special for us and everyone there. Most people cried during the actual marriage ceremony because of the emotions that were evoked by our display of heritage, family union, and happiness.

If you need a visual aid to put together your African-American wedding, a copy of this wedding video can be obtained. The cost is approximately $15. Write or call Ms. Tammey D. Jones, 1338 Madison Street, Americus, Georgia 31709, 1-912-924-3993.

Incredibly beautiful invitations with an African design can be obtained through a new African-American company called Ethnicity, Inc. Each card is hand painted and vividly depicts African culture. The prices are reasonable and comparable to standard invitation book prices. Write or call Ethnicity, Inc., C/O Angela Hill, 9637 South Jeffery Avenue, Chicago, Illinois 60617, 1-800-546-3310 or 1-312-734-3310.

An African-American company is now providing "African wedding broomsticks with carved handles" to facilitate the reenactment of the custom of "Jumping the Broom." Write or call Stewart Ethnic Enterprises, Inc., C/O Beverly Stewart-Linder, 9 South 321 Graceland, Dowers Grove, Illinois 60516, 1-708-910-7770.

Information about African-American wedding dresses can be obtained by writing or calling Mrs. Abenaa Owusu, Agyeiwa's African Boutique, 1429 South Monroe Street, Tallahassee, Florida, 32301, 1-904-656-2700.

African-American Folk Music

African-American Folksongs by Henry E. Krehbiel
St. Helena Island Spirituals by N.G.J. Ballanta
American Negro Folksongs by Newman Ivey White

Popular African-American Spirituals

All God's Children Got Wings
Deep River
Little David Play on Your Harp
Roll, Jordan Roll
Swing Low, Sweet Chariot
You Go, I Go with You
Rise up Shepherd and Follow
Precious Lord, Take My Hand

African-American Musical Instruments

Banjo
Drums
Xylophone (Balafoo)
Gong-gongs
Thumb Piano
Bells
Lute

African-American Dance

"Adinkra," a dance performed by a man and women (Ashanti)

Flowers Native to Africa

Painted Daisy
Bluewings
Cockscomb

To further research the different customs, foods, dress, flowers, and words of your African ancestors, these are some other various West African groups you may want to investigate: Akan, Fon, Yoruba, Ibo, Fanti, Fulani, Ashanti, Joluf, Bakongo, and Baoulé.

❧ Hispanic-American Ceremonies

There are many customs attached to a Hispanic wedding celebration. Here are just a few to activate your imagination.

Laso

A laso an ornate double rosary or a white rope used during the ceremony. After the priest has made the sign of the cross over the heads of each of the couple in turn and they have kissed the cross of the double rosary, the double loops of the "laso" are placed over the shoulders of the couple by a specially designated person or another couple. The laso is frequently draped around the couple in a figure eight and remains in place throughout the entire ceremony to represent the marriage bond. At the end of the marriage ceremony, the laso is removed by the priest or the party that originally placed it over the couple and is given to the bride as a token and keepsake of their marriage ceremony. The ornate double rosary can cost as little as $30 and as much as $100, and is usually given to the couple by one set of parents. In some areas of Hispanic culture, a mantilla may be used in place of the laso. The mantilla is frequently a family heirloom and may be presented by godparents to the couple.

Arriahs

This custom originated in Spain. It consists of the use of 13 small coins, stamped with the words, "in remembrance of the wedding," and represents the dowry of the bride and the good wishes of her family for a prosperous union. In some older cultures, the coins represented the groom's dowry to his bride and held authentic monetary value. The coins are generally contained in a small box or tray. After they have been blessed by the priest, they are poured back and forth from the hands of the bride to that of the groom and again back to the hands of the bride. The custom ends when the coins are returned to their box or tray, which is then placed in the hands of the bride at the conclusion of the ceremony and represents her control of the family finances. Imitations of the 13 gold coins and the small tray or container range in price from $4 to about $15. Gold-plated reproductions are also available and used in affluent Hispanic weddings.

Rings

Rings are presented to the priest for blessing by the person who bought them. Originally, the best man was responsible for the purchase of the wedding rings. Today, it is usually the groom but can also be a relative, or sometimes a combination of funds can be used to purchase the rings.

Flowers

Three bouquets of flowers are used. A small bouquet of real flowers is placed at the feet of a statue of the Virgin Mary by the couple, to honor her during the ceremony. One bouquet is kept by the bride as a wedding keepsake, and a third bouquet is used to throw during the reception celebration. This is known as La Biborita. The Hispanic custom of La Biborita involves both the bride and groom. Single females get up and dance before the bouquet toss while the bride and groom stand on chairs, facing each other. The groom's coat is removed and the couple holds the garment up as an arch for the single women to dance under and around. When the music stops, the bouquet is tossed out to the women by the bride.

Bible

A bible is usually given to the couple by a friend or relative. After it has been blessed by the priest, it becomes the family book of prayer.

Crowns

These are tied together with ribbons and represent the marriage of Adam and Eve. Crowns of metal or wreaths of flowers are placed on the heads of each of the couple and exchanged back and forth during the ceremony. (The ceremony of the crowns is frequently used in Hispanic areas where Greek and Russian Orthodox groups are also present, as this tradition originated with the Orthodox.)

The Ceremony

Honor attendants sometimes read poems and blessings to the couple and their families and may formally escort the bride and the groom to greet each set of parents during the ceremony. The couple may also sign the marriage certificate in front of their witnesses during the ceremony. Communion is received by the couple, their family, and the entire congregation. The mothers of the bride and groom are frequently involved with the serving of the communion by presenting the communion wafer to the priest for blessing beforehand. Hispanic people tend to be family oriented and all members of each family are usually invited to a wedding.

Dress

Brides usually wear white and weddings gowns are very full, with yards and yards of lace ruffles. Bridesmaids, or madrinas, frequently dress in red, which is considered a primary color for Hispanic wedding celebrations. Groomsmen, or padrinos, are usually attired in black tuxedos or suits.

Music and Food

Usually a mixture of music is played during the ceremony and reception. Mariachis are commonly used at the end of the ceremony as the couple leave the church and again during the reception dinner. Mariachi groups of several musicians dressed in colorful red, gold, and black suits with large sombreros perform while strolling about the reception area. Mariachi music can be both festive and romantic. The meal, always a true feast, can consist of traditional foods or a mixture of traditional and American. Music for dancing following the feast is usually Mambo, Salsa, and Cha Cha. Contemporary sounds may also be woven in.

Finances

It is common for many family members to help pay for the cost of Hispanic weddings, and frequently "sponsors" will be listed in the wedding program, along with what they contributed to the ceremony. In some areas of Mexico the groom's family pays for the entire wedding and his best man is still financially responsible for the wedding rings.

If you need assistance with Hispanic wedding traditions, more information can be obtained by calling or writing Ms. Mimi Doke, The Wedding Specialist, 1425 McCulloch Boulevard, Lake Havasu City, Arizona 86403, 1-602-453-6000.

Japanese Ceremonies

Japanese wedding ceremonies can center around ancient traditions that date back thousands of years. Here are a few to begin with if you choose to accent your ceremony with a touch of your Asian past.

Vows. These are composed by the bride and groom and read aloud during the ceremony.

Shinto Priest. He performs the ceremony in front of a shrine.

Sakaki tree. People believe that God lives in the Sakaki tree, and its branches are, therefore, considered holy. Sakaki branches are carried by both the bride and groom. During the marriage ceremony, they are placed in front of the shrine beside the papers on which the couple have written their vows, to bless and sanctify the marriage.

Sansankudo. This is a ceremony in which the bride and groom each drink three times from a cup filled with saki. The word sansankudo translates into "three times three is nine," which is considered a lucky number for the Japanese. The ceremony is done to ensure good luck and a prosperous union.

Cranes. These birds are symbols of Kotobuki, or happiness. and may be used in various decorative modes for the ceremony and reception.

National flowers. Cherry blossoms and chrysanthemum are the national flowers of Japan.

For additional information on Japanese wedding traditions contact Yoriko Baba or Shin Horiuchi, Watabe Wedding Services Ltd., 1-19-4 Kyobashi, Chuoh-ku, Tokyo, Japan, 03-3864-4111 or 03-3564-4111.

✒ Additional Traits and Customs of Various Cultures

If you would like to bring additional accents to your wedding scene from your ancestral past, consider having one or more of your wedding party dressed in the traditional dress of your ancestors. These people could greet your guests as they enter the church for the ceremony, be assigned to collect names for your guest book, or simply mingle with all the guests during the celebration party.

Another possibility would be to use traditional foods, flowers, or dances from your ethnic heritage. Consider talking to your parents, grandparents, or other relatives to get their thoughts on what might be appropriate for your wedding to represent your background. Following are dances and flowers from various lands to get you started.

Countries	Dances		Flowers
Russia	Akron	circle dance	Maltese-cross
	Kolo	square dance	Foster's tulip
	Beseda	circle dance	
Greece	Syrtos	circle dance	Florist's cyclamen
	Tsamiko	handkerchief dance	Yellow foxglove
Spain	Sardona	circle dance	Lily leek
	Flamenco	traditional dance	Miniature daffodil
Denmark	Hatter	square dance	Bell flower
Norway	Song	circle dance	Marsh marigold
Ireland	Sweets of May	circle dance	Heather
Scotland	Eightsome Reel	square dance	Thistle
England	Newcastle	square dance	English bluebell
	Childgrove	contra dance	
Germany	Man in the Hay	square dance	Globeflower
Austria	Schuplatter	traditional dance	Edelweiss
Portugal	Fandango	traditional dance	Carnation
France	La bouree	Celtic jig	French anemone
Italy	Tarantella	traditional dance	Sweet pea
			Mallo
Poland	Holubetz	traditional dance	Spurge
			Dwarf blue iris
Mexico	Mexican hat dance	traditional dance	Dahlia
	Yaqui	Indian deer dance	Yellow cosmos

Countries	Dances		Flowers (continued)
Brazil	Samba	traditional dance	Bush violet (native to S. America)
Columbia	Cueca	traditional dance	Spider flower (native to S. America)
Venezuela	Joroko	traditional dance	Tuberous begonia (native to S. America)
Argentina	Carnavalito	traditional dance	Spring starflower
Chile	Cueca	folk dance	Copihue
			Butterfly flower

See the *Encyclopedia of Flowers* by Derek Fell, published by Smithmark, 1992, for other flowers from various parts of the world.

Ideas for creative and colorful food dishes from your particular culture might be acquired from the multitude of cookbooks that you will find at your local library. Here are a few to explore food culture:

A Taste of Ireland by Theodora Fitzgibbon; Avenel Books

The Celebrity Kosher Cookbook by Marilyn Hall and Rabbi Jerome Cutler; J. P. Tarcher, Inc. 1975

The Spirit of the Harvest North American Indian Cooking by Beverly Cox and Martin Jacobs; Stewart, Tabori and Chang, N.Y. 1991

Hilton International Cookbook by the Hilton Chefs; Prentice-Hall 1960

The Best Italian Cooking by Nika Standen Hazelton; The World Publication Co. 1967

Mastering the Art of French Cooking by Julia Child and Simone Beck; Alfred A. Knoke, Inc. 1970

Time-Life Books, Inc. has done a series of books called *Library of Nations*. This insightful review of the many different parts of the world might provide you with interesting information and materials and food for thought about your ancestry. A review of various encyclopedias may give you further information on your particular culture and its roots. Another quick and easy idea to do a colorful review of various cultures is to peruse the children's section of books at your library on different countries and their cultures.

Chapter Twelve

The Way We Are—Happy and Independent

Creative Wedding Ideas for the Physically Challenged

Physically challenged people are participating in life in many different ways, from winning academy awards for their creative acting ability (Marlee Matlin for *Children Of A Lesser God*), to entering and winning marathons, skiing, and scaling mountains. Independent living with a job, a home of their own, and marriage, is as much of a reality for them today as for any other segment of society. They are also doing wonderful and imaginative things to color and accent their wedding day with pageantry and memories.

❧ "We Could Have Danced All Night!"

Kathy and Bill are two people who enjoy life to the fullest. Kathy is a teacher who has cerebral palsy. Bill, her husband, who has muscular dystrophy, is a technical illustrator. Bill is able to stand but for the most part, both his and Kathy's mobility is directly linked to wheelchair use. "We met and fell in love at a St. Patrick's day party, at an independent living center for the physically challenged. From that day on, there was no looking back for either of us. It was only a matter of time before we began to think about marriage."

The logistics of their wedding had to be well thought out, and there were many details to consider. Finding a priest to perform the ceremony was their first hurdle. Kathy wanted to be married at a local Catholic church close to her apartment, but this was not to be.

I naturally thought of this church first but when I met with the priest to begin to work out the details, he seemed less than receptive to our marriage. He inquired about my age, and if my parents were aware of our desire to marry. He asked me ridiculous questions! Once I understood his unqualified resistance to our union, I simply searched out another priest in another parish and our plans began to move forward.

Wedding apparel presented some additional problems.

I sent my mother out to "scout out" the type of dress I wanted to be married in and then went to the bridal shop to give final approval and do my ordering. I was able to find a seamstress who came to my house to fit my dress and she did a great job of getting the hem to hang even across the bottom of my wheelchair. This was not an easy feat, since CP has caused my stature to be somewhat less than perfect. However, she listened closely to what I wanted her to do and working together like this, my dress fit perfectly and looked beautiful on our wedding day.

One creative idea that Kathy did with her wedding gown was to have her seamstress cut off the back bow and train and attach it to the top of the back of her wheelchair, using a velcro strip.

This accomplished two things. I wanted to do something to cover the back of my motorized chair where the battery is contained, and placing my train over it worked out well. It also allowed me to keep the train of my dress and have it show perfectly as I meandered down the aisle with my parents on each side of me. I asked several wedding consultants for their ideas about hiding my battery but they didn't have very constructive views in this regard. I finally came up with this idea on my own. When you stop to think about it, it just makes common sense.

Kathy had asked Bill if he wanted to stand or sit for the ceremony and he chose to be seated, the same as she. "I wanted to be able to look into Kathy's eyes throughout the ceremony and especially when we took our marriage vows. Being seated seemed natural." (It is interesting to note that in some countries, such as Mexico, all marriage ceremonies are done with the couple seated for the entire event. With couples generally very nervous on their wedding day, perhaps this should be an option for many people to consider.) Bill also requested that the length of his tuxedo pants be measured from his sitting position. "Pant length has to be a little longer for them to come to the top of your shoes when you are in a sitting position. This was a very important point for our photography."

Finding a church and reception hall that was "wheelchair accessible" was another problem they had to reconcile.

We not only had to think of our individual, physically challenged needs, but also those of several of our W/C [wheelchair] friends that we wanted to invite to our wedding. We spoke to each of them in turn and made a list of particular items that would be required for our church and reception site. In this way, we didn't omit something that might have been important to the physical needs of any of these guests.

For the first dance at their celebration party following the wedding ceremony, Kathy's personal care attendant, "my PCA," lifted her onto Bill's lap and they whirled around and around together in his wheelchair, to the sounds of various waltz melodies.

We had talked about how to make this moment special and asked several nieces and nephews to come forward and provide us with sparkling soap bubbles to "dance" through. This added a nice touch and helped us to accent these first magic moments of rapture and happiness. We had asked the kids to keep it a surprise for everyone there, which they did. Our family and guests loved it and the pictures of our "first dance" together as husband and wife, are very pretty with just a hint of little wispy bubbles all around us.

The traditional dance with their parents also presented Kathy and Bill with a dilemma, because they felt that something should be done to honor their families, but were not sure how to do this. They eventually came up with the idea of doing a freeze-frame video using pictures from childhood and of their families. They also included pictures from their dating years that showed how their relationship and love had evolved. Several pieces of their favorite music were used to weave all the photos together. Kathy and Bill are now considering adding on to their dedication video with some of their actual wedding pictures to continue their personal picture story.

We have a wonderful still picture in our wedding album of our family and the two of us viewing our personal video. The faces of everyone in this group truly shows the emotions and pleasure the video evoked. We were able to find a person who worked out of his home to prepare our tape and the cost of our fifteen minute dedication video to our parents, was less than one hundred dollars.

✎ The Eyes Have It

Wedding preparations and ceremonies for the blind person require attention to details regarding sound, touch, smell, and taste. Elaine Parker, a professional wedding consultant from Nashville, Tennessee, related to me a wonderful story of what was done at one wedding that she helped put together for a bride, her five bridesmaids, and the maid of honor, all of whom were blind. "The wedding had over two hundred attending guests and the couple did about everything that is done at most weddings, in spite of the visual challenge for the bride and her blind attendants."

The initial phase was taking them all out to select the wedding apparel. "I worked with a small bridal shop that was more receptive to this party's needs than some of the larger shops." Feeling the various dress and shoe fabrics was important and helped the bride and her attendants conceptualize the apparel and its design.

The next appointment was with the florists. "I wanted the bride to select flowers that smelled beautiful so that she would always associate a particularly wonderful scent with her wedding day. She liked the scent of Stephanotis so we made sure that in addition to her bouquet, this particular bloom was also included in all the other bouquets, boutonnieres, and corsages."

To get the bridesmaids and the bride down the aisle with safety and musical cadence, Elaine had them all rely on the beat of the organ music to maintain a balance to their walk.

> We used music with 4/4 timing and we rehearsed for two-and-one-half hours, until they all felt secure with this. In addition, every part of the wedding was put into braille and on tape. The braille cards gave cues and reminders to the bride and her attendants. The tapes were sent to parents and immediate family members, all of whom were out of town, so that they would all know the rhythm of the wedding and their part in it. In Tennessee, information can be put into braille by volunteer organizations such as prison workers and these are who we used to help us.

The cloth runner that is usually laid out just before the bride walks down the aisle was put down at the very start of the ceremony. "This made it easier for all the bridesmaids to sense their footing in both directions of going down and coming back up the aisle. We also had used a runner at practice to acquaint everyone with the feel of this underfoot."

The groom wanted a candlelight ceremony, since it was a five o'clock wedding. However, "because safety was a realistic concern, we agreed that using lit candles for some of the photography following the ceremony made more sense. Using candles at this point in the wedding plan gave everyone a feeling of control over the danger of fire."

> After the ceremony, each bridesmaid was escorted to the church door area by one of the groomsmen, and a receiving line was set up here. At the

reception, the bride and groom were seated at a small head table with just their parents. The bridesmaids were seated at various tables with their escorts. This made eating very easy and each blind person's meal was set up in a fashion familiar to them.

The wedding was well thought out and rehearsed so that it went off with out any surprises or undue problems.

☙ A Sign of the Times

Signing and using two interpreters at their wedding helped Linda and Brian have a very beautiful and happy wedding day.

> We did everything, through the use of our interpreters, that hearing people do at traditional wedding scenes. Both of us are deaf but we do not consider ourselves "impaired" in any way. When we started to plan for our wedding, we pretty much followed along the usual routes for preparing for a large church wedding. Shopping for the wedding apparel was accomplished without any undue stress because I was able to work through a small bridal shop that was more attuned to our needs than perhaps a larger one might have been.

> We were married in a Catholic church and found the priest most receptive and helpful. He did not sign, but through the use of an interpreter we made our needs known to him and prepared him to do our wedding service. It was most important for us to be comfortable with the person who was going to perform our ceremony, as with any other couple getting married. We were fortunate to find a cleric that was helpful, understanding and fun to work with right from the start of it all.

Communication was, of course, an important part of their wedding plan, and it flowed very easily through the use of interpreters. "During the ceremony we used two interpreters. One for sign communications to our deaf friends attending the ceremony, and another for vocal communication for the rest of our hearing family and invited guests.

At the reception, most of the traditional things were done.

> Having an interpreter beside us during the receiving line was important of course. During the meal, instead of people tapping their glasses with their spoons when they wanted to cue us to kiss each other, they all waved their napkins at Brian and me and this worked very well. One of the things that I do wish that I had done differently was to reserve a table closer to the front of the room for our deaf guests. My mother and I forgot to mention this

when we contracted for the banquet room. I think it was hard for some of them to see us where they were seated. Having them seated closer to us at the front of the room would have given them more visual input as to what was going on at the head table. This would have been better for them.

Linda had her mother select the music for the ceremony and reception because "music is not important to either Brian or me. However, there are different degrees of deafness and the type of music used at some weddings involving deaf people might be an important feature for other semi deaf individuals or couples."

✒ Some Additional Ideas

Here are just a few more ideas for physically challenged, deaf, or blind brides and grooms to consider using at their wedding ceremony or celebration party:

1. *Ask each invited guest to bring a long-stemmed silk flower to the ceremony and assign a certain person to collect them at the church door. Provide him or her with green florist's tape and a roll of pretty ribbon. While you are having your photography done following your ceremony, have this person wrap the flowers together with the tape and ribbon, into a giant flower lei. For your first "dance" at your reception, have your best man and maid of honor encircle the two of you and your wheelchairs with the lei. In Hawaii, the flower lei is the symbol of love and greeting, and the circle is the symbol of eternity.*

2. *If you are visually impaired, get married near a waterfall or at the ocean. The sound of rushing water or the smell of salt air anywhere you go from this day forward will always remind you of your wedding day.*

3. *Have the sign language sign for love incorporated into your monogram and use it on the front of your invitation. Use the sign for love to create your wedding cake, or repeated again and again as part of the frosting design.*

4. *Have clothing patches made to show the love sign if your are deaf and use them as wedding favors at your reception. Attach a small bow to each, using your wedding colors.*

5. *Assign each immediate family member the task of telling a short story from your youth. Conclude the stories with your own special stories of*

how you met your spouse. *This can be woven into your ceremony or done at your celebration party.*

6. *Incorporate braille into your invitation and ceremony program wording. Spray your invitations with the scent of the flowers that you plan to use at your wedding.*

7. *Decorate the spokes of the wheels on your wheelchairs by weaving ribbons in and out of them, and place wedding streamers on the handles of your chairs.*

8. *If you are going to have attendants that are vision impaired, have a flower girl or boy for each one, to assist them down the aisle. If your bridesmaids are dressed in print dresses, dress each "assistant" in a different color of the print to accent each individual bridesmaid.*

9. *If you ambulate with crutches, decorate them with flowers and ribbons and have decorated chairs to sit on during your marriage ceremony.*

10. *If you are deaf, use bold colors for all your flowers, attendants' dresses, or as accessories, and decorations to shout out your happiness to all your guests, and as vivid reminders of your wedding day.*

11. *Attach small, silvery sounding wedding bells to all the floral arrangements so that they can be heard, as well as seen, throughout your wedding day.*

12. *Use material that is readily discernible through your sense of touch such as a velvet for your wedding dress and tuxedo jacket.*

13. *Have bookmarks done in braille, using a favorite saying or poem, and use these as your favors at the reception.*

14. *If you use an animal to assist you with your daily living needs, have a bow, flower corsage, or lei made for him or her to wear at your wedding. Include his or her name in your wedding program.*

15. *Hire an ice cream truck to make an "unexpected" visit at your celebration party to give your guests some additional "good humor" through their acute sense of sound, sight, smell, taste, and touch.*

See chapter 15 for additional ideas on expressions of wedding-day joy and remembrance.

Chapter Thirteen

Away-From-Home Weddings: "Don't Worry—Be Happy!"

If thinking about the traditional wedding scene, large or small, feels overwhelming or uncomfortable, perhaps it is simply not the right approach for you. Couples might feel this way for a variety of reasons. They may be older when they decide to marry. It may be a second marriage for one or both of them. Too many family members and friends may make the task of setting a realistic guest list impossible. The family situation may be complicated, or the families may be unwilling to come together without a big fuss.

An intimate, wedding service may be closer to the right style for you. Trying to accomplish this at home is difficult. Weddings seem to grow in size and complexity, no matter how the design is originally conceived. You may feel pressure from family and friends who can't be invited due to the very nature of this type of wedding. Because of this, the guest list starts to grow. More and more details then have to be considered and addressed. Your wedding plans for an intimate ceremony begin to take on the picture of the large wedding you were hoping to avoid.

If this scenario strikes a nerve with you and your future mate, perhaps having a wedding away from home would suit you better. Each year, thousands of couples elect to be married in far-off locations for these very reasons. Or they may simply decide to use their resources to honeymoon, rather than entertain a large crown of friends and relatives. Unlike eloping, this approach is more formal and open. It can provide a very romantic beginning for marriage. All in all, this idea carries a very positive connotation.

Because the ceremony is held at a distant location, setting the guest list is certainly easier. A few close family members and friends might be invited along to witness the event. For some couples, the idea of being married without family and friends is a barrier. However, because people are so widely dispersed, air travel may be a necessity in any event. Couples have been surprised to find that a good number of people may elect to accompany them to their wedding destination. Those that choose to attend the wedding ceremony are responsible for their own travel and expense, of course.

Spectacular locations for the wedding ceremony that would ingratiate a king and queen are readily available. Because of its charm and reliable climate, the Caribbean seems more than perfect. Classic European courtesy and island traditions weave a romantic and colorful tapestry. Horse-drawn carriages, white sand beaches with emerald- and turquoise-colored water, exotic flowers, and gentle trade winds are the norm. Moonlit, enchanting nights, filled with soft steel band music and scents of lush tropical foliage, set a bewitching scene for lovers here.

The more adventuresome couple might consider being married at the bottom of the Grand Canyon. An exciting white water rafting trip brings them to the wedding site, complete with waterfall and native flowers.

For the couple that really wants to go far away, the South Pacific might suit. An exotic wedding, complete with traditional dress for the bride and groom, is available in the Fiji islands. You may entertain thoughts of getting married on safari in Africa to the sounds of tribal music and dancing. Europe, with its old world charm and romantic castles, should also enter into your considerations for an "away-from-home" wedding.

A couple with more tender hearts may entertain thoughts of a wedding ceremony in New England when the hills are embraced with the unsurpassed colors of fall. If you are a serious skier and want to marry in a Swiss Alps atmosphere without leaving the United States, Vail, Colorado may be the answer. This storybook community comes equipped with a little chapel, ideal for an intimate ceremony.

The cost is not necessarily unreasonable. Wedding ceremonies start at about $500, depending on size, location, and design. Of course, air and hotel are additional, but remember that this is for your honeymoon as well.

Selecting wedding apparel is often times easier and less expensive with this wedding option. Many brides choose an informal gown simply because it fits in so well with the lovely ceremony settings. However, here, too, brides and grooms often select the traditional wedding garb. Couples have been photographed taking their vows on the beach or on a mountain top in full regalia of tuxedo and long, flowing gown, complete with train.

Lead time for an away-from-home wedding is usually about four to six weeks. This does depend somewhat on the selected destination and time of year, but in comparison to the typical at-home wedding, very little time is required to set your plans in motion. Even Catholic ceremonies are possible.

More time is needed to arrange these ceremonies due to the church's requirements. In particular, Catholic weddings must take place inside the church, but some areas offer beautiful old cathedrals to this end.

Upon returning home, announcements of your recent wedding can be sent out to family and friends and all can be invited to a reception celebration with one stroke of the pen. It can be formal or informal. Plans for a reception party following an away wedding are pressure-free and relatively easy and inexpensive to put together. You may be surprised to receive several such parties during your first year of marriage, as you visit distant relatives or close friends. An away-from-home wedding is not for everyone, but can be an option for many.

⁓ Wedding License Requirements

Each U.S. state and foreign country has different marriage license requirements. In general, there are several items that will be required anywhere and some items that may be needed in addition, depending on the location selected for the marriage ceremony. These are:

Passports or Birth Certificates*
Photo ID*
Divorce Decree*
Residency Requirement and/or Waiting Period*
Death Decree of Previous Spouse*
Tourist Card
Blood Tests
Health Certificates
Posting of Marriage Banns
Joint or Separate Property Statements

All documents must be certified with a raised seal and must be translated into English.

Before ceremony plans can be made, license requirements must be dealt with. Because laws and governments change, updated information should be

---

* These are the general requirements for obtaining a wedding license in most places. Residency requirements and/or waiting periods vary from zero to three days in most cases.

acquired within the state or country where the ceremony is to take place. This is done by:

1. *Locating the proper arm of government in the state or country where you desire to be married. For the United States, call the city hall or a town office of the county where the marriage is to take place. For a foreign country, call their embassy in Washington, D.C., to get information on which branch of government handles marriage licensing. Contact that branch by phone or in writing.*
2. *Be absolutely sure about residency requirements, waiting periods, health requirements, documentation requirements, and holidays particular to the area you plan to be married in. These things, not properly understood, can unexpectedly delay marriage plans.*
3. *Always recheck license requirements prior to departure. Be positive that all required documents are authentic and certified, showing a raised seal.*

Several possible destinations are examined on the following pages. Each is unique in its own way. These are but a few of the lovely places that you might use for your wedding ceremony. They offer different romantic flavors to suit various lifestyles and budgets. They have been selected as ideas for you to use or as a jumping-off point leading to other exotic, exciting, and memorable wedding places.

◈ Tying the Knot at Sea

For those who love ships and sailing, one of the most romantic wedding services available is that of the Windjammer Barefoot Cruises. They offer a wedding service aboard two of their ships, the S/V Flying Cloud (British Virgin Island Wedding) and the S/V Fantome (Bahamas Wedding). Each is a majestic tall ship. You and your gang can even stow away on ship the night before she sails (approximately $35 per person.) Marriages can be arranged at several different islands.

To obtain a license to marry in the British Virgin Islands or the Bahamas, you must be age 21 or older and present the following:

1. *Passports or birth certificates*
2. *If either has previously been married, a certified or notarized copy of the divorce decree*

The wedding takes place at about five in the evening, several days into the cruise. Several more days are spent honeymooning aboard while sailing to visit Drakes Passage, Treasure Isles, and other Caribbean jewels. "Cooking, steel band parties, sightseeing, shopping, masquerade parties, snorkeling and relaxing with your new life mate and friends fill up the days and nights." The ships' galleys prepare wonderful meals of home-cooked soups, fish, and island specialties. Lunch is usually a beach picnic or buffet. Even an evening snack is prepared each night, to be enjoyed under the stars while soft trade winds keep you cool and comfortable.

The fees for a license, officiator, and Windjammer wedding ceremony are approximately U.S. $265. Flowers, champagne, and fantastic food make each wedding ceremony an unforgettable experience. Cruise prices for the winter season are approximately $1650 per couple. The honeymoon suite is available at about $2250 per couple. There are only one or two of these suites on each ship and they should be booked 18 months in advance to assure availability. A quick note or call to their telephone number will get you all the information and details for this memorable wedding and honeymoon aboard a tall and majestic sailing ship. For more information, contact Windjammer Barefoot Cruises, Ltd., P.O. Box 120, Miami Beach, Florida 33119, 1-800-327-2601 or 1-305-672-6453.

✒ Saying "I Do" at the Bottom, or Top, of the Grand Canyon

For a most exciting, dramatic, and memorable wedding ceremony, consider a "world class river trip" down the Colorado River. At various camp sites along the way, you can stand side by side and speak your marriage vows to one another, surrounded by beautiful and scenic rock walls and water falls that are over two billion years old. Getting to one of these lovely spots along the great river is an unforgettable experience in itself, as you ride down the rapids in several large motor driven pontoon boats and feel "the river's pummeling energy."

Canyoneers, Inc., of Flagstaff, Arizona, is an authorized concessionaire of the National Park Service, and has been providing white water boating trips since 1970. You will experience warm camaraderie, wonderful food, and comfortable sleeping arrangements under the stars. The fee for a 7 day trip down the river is $1400 per person; if you want to be married at a special spot along the way, other than the customary donation for the officiator, there is no extra fee for the service. The ceremony is legally authorized by using one of your crew, who is also a minister, to perform your marriage service.

If you would like to just look into the Grand Canyon, rather than experience the white-water river ride down the mighty Colorado, a winter wedding can be arranged for you at their North Rim Nordic Center. This is a "winter wonderland" ski lodge, located near the North Rim of the Grand Canyon. Here there are many beautiful scenic locations for a romantic and memorable ceremony and a cozy lodge to give you all the creature comforts one could hope for. For further details and information on arranging one of these two wedding ceremonies, write or call Canyoneers, Inc., P.O. Box 2997, Flagstaff, Arizona 86003, 1-800-525-0924 or 1-602-526-0924.

❧ St. Kitts, West Indies

Located in the northern part of the Leeward Islands of the West Indies, close to the equator, St. Kitts is 23 miles long and includes a rugged mountain range and dormant volcano. British, French, and African heritage give the island a colorful and festive spirit. The Golden Lemon, a superior first class inn, offers a wedding ceremony for its guests for a fee of $500 that includes the following:

Marriage license
Minister and witnesses
Wedding bouquet
Cake
Wedding certificate
A wedding night dinner

Photography is additional. Note that the waiting period for obtaining a marriage license on this island is two full working days.

"The resort features individual villas with their own pools, and incredibly beautiful views. Magnificently decorated sea view bedrooms in the Great House overlook elegant gardens." Fine Creole, Continental, and American cuisine with "afternoon tea" make this resort special. Snorkeling at a nearby reef and horseback riding are also available. A seven day stay at this lovely location will range in price, depending on your type of accommodations and time of year, from about $2300-$2800 per couple plus tax, and includes daily breakfast and a candlelight dinner each night. For approximately $3800 you can rent a villa, equipped with a private pool. For more information on this unforgettable marriage ceremony, write or call The Golden Lemon, Dieppe Bay, St. Kitts, West Indies, 1-809-465-7260 or 1-800-633-7411.

⟿ U.S. Virgin Islands Nuptials

Reverend Drew Wallen is a minister in the Universal Life Church and has been marrying couples who come to St. Thomas for many years now. His wife Patty helps with the arrangements, and also is available as a witness if you don't care to bring your own. Wallen can marry you at just about any hotel property on the island or on one of the many beautiful beaches found here. Most of the hotels will charge you for using their grounds for a marriage ceremony unless you are a registered guest. Bluebeard's Castle, however, is an exception. There is also no charge for using any one of St. Thomas' white sand beaches, if you wish to have your ceremony "on the beach" with an emerald green ocean in the background.

Wedding ceremonies in the U.S. Virgin Islands can be arranged for a fee of about $400 and up, depending on "how many ruffles you want to add on to your ceremony!" A basic design would include license, minister, flowers, music, and transportation to the wedding site. Photography and video are available at about $150 for each service.

"Jumping ship" to be married is another choice that is available with the Reverend Wallen's services. The Wallens will arrange to meet you after your cruise ship docks, take you to pick up the marriage license, and then on to the romantic wedding site of your choice for the ceremony. For an additional fee, ceremonies can also be arranged on the serene and beautiful nearby island of St. John, a short boat ride away.

No blood tests are required and all the licensing preliminaries can be handled by mail. The application can be obtained from your local Virgin Islands tourist office and should be mailed in at least four weeks in advance. Once you arrive on the island, the license must be signed for in person, but then you are free to marry at once.

To obtain the latest information on being married in the U.S. Virgin Islands, write or call Reverend Drew Wallen, Island Photo Service, P.O. Box 9979, St. Thomas, V.I., 00801, 1-809-779-2141 or 1-800-937-1346.

☙ Fiji—A "Blue Lagoon" Paradise for Your Ceremony

Getting married on beautiful Turtle Island, a 500-acre island in the Yasawa group of the Fijian islands, located in the South Pacific, is an unforgettable experience. The resort there is small, only 14 "bures," or thatched roof cottages, set the on famous Blue Lagoon, of motion picture fame. Lush landscaping and four-poster beds with lace canopy netting make these superior, first class, beachside accommodations elegant and romantic. There are also 14 white sand private beaches, or one for each couple if you like.

The pace on Turtle Island is slow and relaxing and the Fijian people friendly and fun loving. All food, drink, and water activities are included in the cost of your stay. "Meals consist of a sumptuous gourmet menu of crab, lobster, Australian beef, fresh vegetables and tropical island fruits." Fijian music and dancing under the stars are nightly events.

The wedding scene could begin at sunset on the shores of Blue Lagoon, with conch shell sounds announcing the bride's arrival on a wedding raft decorated with flowers. She is escorted to her groom by two Fijian attendants and a choir of native music then leads the couple to the marriage altar. Traditional Fijian wedding attire is optional if you don't want to bother with European-styled wedding duds purchased at home. A pig roast is then held to celebrate the new marriage, under the soft glow of lantern lights and a sky filled with Fijian stars.

The marriage license is applied for and picked up in one step upon arrival in Lautoka, before you are flown by private plane out to Turtle Island. The wedding usually takes place about three days after arrival. The fee for the ceremony is approximately $1000, which includes the minister, music, food, video, photography, cake, and the bride and groom's traditional Fijian wedding dress. A seven night, all-inclusive stay on Turtle Island will cost about $5000 per couple. For more information about getting married in Fiji write or call Turtle Holidays, Quad 205 Complex, 10906 NE 39th St. A-1, Vancouver, Washington 98682, 1-800-826-3083 or 1-206-256-4347.

☙ Antigua—Caribbean Weddings

Pronounced "An-tee-ga," this Eastern Caribbean island is partly coral and partly volcanic, with a plethora of white-sand beaches (365, or one for each day of the year!). The Blue Waters Beach Hotel offers first-class accommodations and can arrange a truly memorable wedding. You can exchange vows in a cliff-top gazebo, overlooking the sea, with a garden reception at poolside if you wish. Included in the fee of approximately $700 are the following: license, minister, flowers, wedding cake, photographer, and champagne. All your requests will be taken care of, with great attention to detail, by the hotel's diligent staff.

Obtaining your wedding license on this beautiful island is easy. There are no blood tests needed, and only a short three-day waiting period is required to process the papers. Your ceremony can take place immediately upon obtaining the marriage license.

Set in one of the loveliest and most sheltered areas of the island, the hotel boasts of two palm-fringed, white sand beaches with all the excitement and relaxation one could wish for—sailing, windsurfing, snorkeling, fishing, and nightly dancing under the stars. Golf and casinos are nearby. Afternoon tea and cakes are complimentary. An open air Garden Terrace dining room takes in the blue Caribbean and lush flora and fauna of the private grounds. A seven night stay will range in cost from $980 to $1645 per couple, depending on the time of year and your choice of accommodations. A "room upgrade" and honeymoon breakfast are additional features of this hotel. More information about being married in beautiful Antigua can be obtained by writing or calling Blue Waters Beach Hotel, P.O. Box 256, St. John, Antigua, West Indies, 1-800-372-1323 or 1-081-367-5175.

☞ Moonlight (and Weddings) in Vermont

The Green Mountain State of Vermont has many little villages and towns with a true New England quaintness that is warm and inviting. One exceptional place is the Inn at Essex. Located in the picturesque town of Essex Junction, in the northern part of the state, it can provide you with a romantic atmosphere for marriage. The Inn at Essex is rated superior first class, and the weddings performed here range from large and formal to small and informal. "We are happy to perform marriages of all sizes and can provide a beautiful service for just the two of you or as many as one hundred and fifty invited guests if you desire."

There are several sites that set the scene for a very memorable wedding ceremony.

For an indoor wedding, we have a richly decorated, very cozy library. A large, glowing fireplace with its mantel decorated with flowers and greenery, provides a very special setting for an intimate marriage ceremony on a cold and snowy wintry day. There is also a wonderful circular staircase that is perfect for wedding photography. During the warmer months, our east lawn with its many colorful flower beds is spectacular. There is a large brick patio area here with white tables and chairs and a dance floor. It incorporates a lovely white canopy with roll down sides and windows, to provide a protective and pretty shelter if the weather should call for this.

All fees for wedding services are nominal. The nightly cost of rooms at the Inn will vary from $88 to $158 per couple, depending on the season. Some have a fireplace. The Inn is also the home of the New England Culinary Institute. Each meal is prepared under the direction of a renowned French chef. "The menu at Butler's, one of our on-site restaurants, is like reading from a page out of Gourmet Magazine."

Vermont's largest city, Burlington, and Lake Champlain, the state's largest lake, are only 15 miles down the road. Festive nightlife, cultural activities at the University of Vermont, and scenic boat excursions on the beautiful lake, enclosed by mountains, are some of the exciting entertainment to be found here.

The laws for securing a license to marry in Vermont have recently been changed and there is no longer a waiting period. If your papers are in order when you apply for your license, it can be issued to you at once. It is legal to be married in this state immediately upon receiving your license. The fee is $16 and it can be secured from the town clerk's office, in Essex Junction, Vermont, Monday through Friday from 8 A.M. to 4:30 P.M. The license is valid for 60 days from date of issue and must be used in the same county where it is secured. More information about being married in Vermont at the Inn at Essex can be obtained by writing or calling The Inn at Essex, 70 Essex Way, Essex Junction, Vermont 05452, 1-800-727-4295 or 1-802-878-1100.

✎ Rocky Mountain High Weddings

If you love the mountains and want a spectacular setting for your ceremony, why not get married in Vail, Colorado, amid the Great Rocky Mountains? The Vail Athletic Club has many wonderful places for a memorable ceremony. "We've done weddings on our lovely deck with the scenic mountains as a backdrop and out on our spacious lawns, surrounded with profusions of flowers. There is also pretty Gore creek that runs through the property and provides a special spot for wedding vows. A covered bridge is close by for innovative wedding photography if desired." There is a beautiful chapel within a short distance from the club, in the center of town, and it is ideal for small weddings. A white, horse-drawn carriage is available to carry you, just like Cinderella, through this fairytale town, to and from the chapel for your marriage ceremony.

Hotel accommodations range from traditional rooms to studios with fireplaces. Rates will depend on the season and range from a low of about $115 per night in summer to $355 per night during the Christmas season. A full breakfast and use of the club's extensive equipment is included. An indoor pool, jacuzzis both indoor and outdoor, and various spa services are additional features of this deluxe hotel.

Kristin Goddard of "Bridal Belles" can set up both small and large wedding services and will help you make the necessary arrangements for securing a license to marry in Vail. Both people must be present to apply and sign for the license. Proof of age and a copy of a divorce decree is required, if it occurred during the previous six months. The license is approximately $20 and there is no waiting period. It is valid for 30 days. For more information write or call The Vail Athletic Club, 352 East Meadow Drive, Vail, Colorado 81657, 1-800-822-4754 or 1-303-476-0700 and Wedding Bells, 2121 North Frontage Road, Suite 24, Vail, Colorado 81657, 1-303-949-6064.

⤳ Bermuda Wedding Bells

A group of islands and cays only one-and-a-half hours flight time form Boston, Bermuda will present you with another world: beautiful pastel colored resorts and inns, lush tropical flowers and foliage, "pink sand" beaches, and sparkling turquoise blue water at every turn of the road. Horsedrawn carriages, gourmet restaurants, shops filled with treasures, and the romance of true British tradition await the bride and groom to be.

There are so many lovely places to say "I do" in Bermuda that it is hard to pick just one. Deborah Correia of Wedding Fantasies can help you to sort it all out. She can recommend many picturesque island locations or set your ceremony up at your choice of hotels. Wedding designs start at about $500 and include the license, minister, and photographer. Debbie's consultant fee is an additional 15 percent. A top-notch plan, costing about $1000, will get you your license, minister, photographer, flowers, cake, horse and carriage, and champagne.

You can obtain a "Notice of Intended Marriage" from Wedding Fantasies or the Bermuda Department of Tourism in your area and mail it to the Registrar General, in Hamilton, Bermuda. There is a 14 day waiting period before a license to marry can be issued, as the law in this country requires that marriage banns must be posted. The paperwork can all be done ahead of time however, and the license picked up on your arrival to the island.

A very inexpensive ceremony can also be arranged at the Registry General itself. "Jumping ship" (your cruise ship) and marrying in Bermuda is not difficult to do with Debbie's guidance and help. For more information on getting married at a lovely setting in Bermuda, either while a guest of one of the beautiful hotels on the island, or during your cruise ship's port of call, write or call Ms. Deborah Correia, Wedding Fantasies, P.O. Box HM 729, Hamilton, Bermuda HM CX, 1-809-238-8021.

❧ A Castle Marriage in the City of Mozart

Arranging your marriage ceremony in Salzburg, Austria, is easy to do at the beautiful and romantic Monchstein Castle, built in 1358. Rated superior first class, it is located in the heart of the old inner city, on a large mountain top park, surrounded by the Apollo Gardens. The castle hotel has received several prestigious awards for service and food. Concerts are performed here on Saturdays and Sundays. The home of Mozart, the theater, summer water sports, and winter skating are nearby. A lovely honeymoon suite is available for newlyweds with breakfast included. Room rates start at approximately U.S. $175 per night, and will depend on the season and your choice of accommodations.

An authentic and very beautiful wedding chapel is contained within the castle walls and has served as the setting for many wedding ceremonies from times long ago to the present day. All ceremonies are individual and arranged according to your specifications for a nominal fee. Flowers, cake and wedding photography is approximately U.S. $400. The wedding chapel fee is approximately U.S. $260.

Arranging a wedding in Austria will require about six weeks time as the marriage banns must be posted for several weeks in this country before a marriage ceremony can lawfully take place. All the paperwork can be done ahead of time and upon your arrival, the marriage license is secured.

If you desire more information on being married in Austria at the Monchstein Castle, write or call Hotel Scholss Monchstein, c/o Mr. Hubert

Hirz, General Manager, Monchsberg Park 26-IB, 5020 Salzburg, Austria, 011-43-662-848-5550.

For marriage license information in Salzburg, contact Magistrat Der Stadt Salzburg, Postfach 63, A-5024 Salzburg, Austria, 011- 43- 662-8072 Ext. 2382.

◆ Spanish Bay Reef Weddings—Cayman Islands

The Cayman Islands, composed of three small islands located just south of Cuba, offers the serious diver and the not-so-serious diver, aqua colored waters renowned for their beautiful sea life. Getting married in this lush setting is made possible at the intimate, friendly resort, known as Spanish Bay Reef. It is tucked away on the northwestern tip of Grand Cayman, the largest of the three islands. It offers a private coral beach and comfortable accommodations that are all inclusive. Meals, entertainment, and just about anything else you can think of is included with your stay at the resort. A fully equipped dive shop makes exploration of many nearby charted dive sites possible for both the experienced and novice diver. Use of both scuba and snorkeling equipment is included with your accommodations.

There is a three day waiting period to obtain a marriage license in the Cayman Islands and weddings can be easily arranged through Cayman Weddings. A coordinator will meet with you directly at Spanish Bay Reef Hotel and help with obtaining a marriage license and discuss your personal requests for flowers, photography, etc. The groom's tuxedo can even be rented on the island for about U.S. $80 if you can give them a week's notice.

The cost of a small intimate wedding starts at about U.S. $450 U.S. and includes license, stamp, officiator, flowers, champagne, and cake. Photography and video are extra, but there are several photographers available on the island to choose from. Music is also optional. Renewal of wedding vows is another item to consider for parents of the bride and groom if they plan to accompany you to this romantic wedding site.

"Spanish Bay Reef was once a pirate's haven in bygone days, when Blackbeard and Morgan scoured the Spanish Main for King Phillip's gold and treasure." Today it is a tranquil hideaway that will make your wedding ceremony unforgettable in every way. For more details on planning your ceremony here, write of call Spanish Bay Reef, Attn. Ruth Meerkamp-Smith, P.O. Box

903, Grand Cayman B.W.I., 1-809-949-3765 or Cayman Weddings P.O. Box 678, Grand Cayman, B.W.I., 1-809-949-8677.

✎ Safari Weddings

If you would like to take your nuptial vows at "one of the world's most atmospheric and captivating locations," consider being married while on photographic safari in Africa. Margaret Sanko and Heidi Patty are certified travel consultants and directors of International Ventures of Wilton, Connecticut. Together, they have 20 years of combined special interest travel. They can arrange your ceremony at one of the many beautiful and highly rated accommodations in Nairobi, Kenya.

Weddings can be arranged at several places along the photographic safari route, but one of the loveliest is at Mount Kenya Cathedral, which provides magnificent views of majestic mountains and many exotic birds. There are also several game reserves that you will visit on your wedding trip, teaming with wildlife of every kind. Elephants, giraffe, rhinos, zebras, gazelles, and other wild animals are among those you can view in their natural habitats. (Imagine your wedding photography with some of this splendid wildlife as part of your background scenery!)

The fee for getting to Africa and arranging a marriage ceremony there is approximately U.S. $3000 per person. The 10-day trip includes round trip air from New York to London to Africa, all transfers and accommodations, most meals, game park fees, assistance with wedding license, wedding cake, and ceremony. Photography, video, music, horse-drawn carriage, and other options are also available at very nominal fees. A breakfast at the home portrayed in the movie Out of Africa is an additional option for the day following your marriage ceremony.

For more information on the different sites for a safari wedding from people who have made frequent trips there and will be very attentive to your wedding request and details, write or call Margaret or Heidi at International Ventures Ltd., 65B Old Ridgefield Road, Wilton, Connecticut 06897, 1-800-727-5475 or 1-203-761-1110.

✎ Middlethorpe Hall, York, England

Middlethorpe Hall was built in 1699 and has been skillfully restored to the William III country house it once was. "Its decorations, antiques, and fine pictures have all been carefully chosen as consistent with the period of the house." It is a small, intimate hotel of only 30 guest rooms. The bedrooms are individually decorated and some include a fireplace and/or canopy beds. The lovely estate is set on 26 acres of gardens and includes a small lake.

The city of York is but one mile away. One of the most historic cities of the British Isles, it is still surrounded by beautiful medieval stone walls that are inviting for visitors to walk on. Strolling along the stone walls enables the visitor to see and feel what life must have been like here during the Middle Ages. Within the city, there is the medieval street known as "the Shambles," a castle, several museums, and beautiful York Minster, the largest medieval Gothic cathedral in Northern Europe. "The County of Yorkshire is full of romantic and historic places to see and visit. The countryside is renowned for the beauty of the Yorkshire Dales, and the open splendors of the North York Moors, the Howardian Hills and the exciting coastal scenery."

An attentive staff at Middlethorpe Hall will help with all your wedding arrangements and can easily secure whatever you desire for your ceremony. The cost of a license, minister, small cake, flowers, and photographer is nominal. The license procedure requires a processing period of two-and-a-half weeks, so your planned trip to England should be no less than three weeks time. Your ceremony would take place at the end of your stay in York. For further information regarding a wedding ceremony in England, write or call Mr. S. J. Browning, Manager, Middlethorpe Hall, Bishopthorpe Road, York Y02 1QB, England, 011-090 -464 -1241.

✎ San Antonio Weddings

La Mansion del Rio, located on the famed River Walk in San Antonio, Texas, can provide several very memorable locations for your wedding vows. The hacienda-like hotel is complemented by the winding and romantic River Walk path that stretches across its doorstep. Because of the frontier history attached to this building's past, the hotel has been recognized as a national historical treasure. Old-world ambiance is woven into all aspects of its architecture and the warmth of the personal service you will receive here as a guest of this grand hotel.

"Wedding ceremonies are performed in our secluded and private court-yard which incorporates a Spanish fountain area as the backdrop for your marriage vows. We have also had couples that have chosen to be married on the pretty stone bridge that passes over the River Walk just outside our door-way." A lovely and graceful Cassurina tree provides shade and the arched bridge is draped with beautiful foliage to further enhance the setting. A little stone mission church of historical significance is nearby and some couples choose to be married there.

A romantic boat ride down the pretty and winding river that follows the River Walk is sometimes employed as part of the celebration party following a marriage ceremony. The walk is lined with beautiful shops, enticing restaurants, and other places of historical interest.

> A boat ride along our beautiful River Walk is a fun and exciting way to add to any wedding day celebration, small or large. We will decorate the boat with colorful balloons and arrange for a champagne toast during your ride down the river if your desire. We can provide a memorable wedding ceremony and celebration party for just the bride and groom or one that involves as many as eighty people.

Marriage ceremonies can be performed by a minister or by a justice of the peace. The services of an officiator will cost about $80 to $90 and the courtyard rental fee at La Mansion del Rio is $150. A photographer, cake, and other fees for service are nominal and all available at your request. A short three-day waiting period is required to secure a marriage license in San Antonio. For more information write or call La Mansion del Rio, c/o "Zoe" Banquet Manager, 112 College Street, San Antonio, Texas 78205, 1-800-531-7208 or 1-512-225-2581.

❧ Apparel for Away Weddings

Your wedding attire for a distant ceremony can be formal or informal. It is entirely up to you, the bride and groom. Because the ceremony takes place at a spectacular setting, formal attire of long satin gown with train and a tux, will fit in well. If you wish to eliminate the expense of formalwear, consider a tea-length dress of white, ivory, or pastel color for the bride, and a casual suit for the groom. Again, because of the beautiful ceremony setting, couples look and feel special on their wedding day even when dressed in informal wedding attire.

Modern-day fabric blends allow for easy packing, and wrinkles should not be a big worry. Usually an iron or hand steamer is available from the hotel should your wedding clothes need some minor attention before the ceremony.

For some couples that are conserving their funds, a new set of everyday clothes that can be worn again may be the answer to the question of what to wear. The bride may choose a wedding suit and the groom a new shirt, tie, and slacks. Once flowers are added, this look can also take on a "wedding look" with a beautiful and romantic ceremony setting.

✎ Wedding Travel Advisory

Before you depart, there are a few things you should be aware of to make your plans flow more smoothly. The following information has been gathered from other couples that had their wedding ceremonies at distant locations, and from facilitators at various resorts. It focuses on what has worked best. It encourages you to build your away wedding and honeymoon design around proven ideas.

Your wedding rings should be packed away in a carry-on case, if you are planning to fly. The bride and groom's wedding attire should also be carried onto the plane. The clothing can be carried in a clothing protector bag and can be safely hung in the plane, near your seat.

Witnesses can be provided by the resort or coordinator with whom you have contracted. They will need to know in advance if you plan to bring your own attendants or if they are to provide them for you. This should be included in the cost of the ceremony.

A tuxedo for your groom can be rented from a local supplier wherever you may decide to go. An exception might occur if the area is small and remote. In this case, if a tuxedo is desired by your groom, simply rent one and take it with you. Usually, an extra rental fee will be added on for each additional week the tux is used.

Have reservations made at a special place for your wedding night dinner. This is the time to go really first class in dining out: gourmet dining, a table for two at the water's edge, candlelight, soft music, and impeccable unhurried service. Some resorts will include this in their wedding designs. Be sure to check with the wedding coordinator or hotel manager.

For weddings out of the country, plan to be married mid-week. Marriage licenses generally cannot be obtained on weekends, and many resorts have problems securing an officiator to perform the ceremony on Saturday or Sunday.

Many areas offer limousine, or horse and buggy transportation to the site where the marriage is to be performed. This can add a very romantic and exciting beginning to your ceremony and should be considered as an option.

If you plan to have your ceremony at an inn somewhere, rent rooms for yourselves and your guests for the weekend. This assures you the innkeepers' undivided attention and more privacy for your wedding ceremony.

Set aside some funds to purchase something from your honeymoon experience for your home, to keep honeymoon memories alive.

Ask about a return trip. Many places will offer a reduced room rate for the second time around.

If you take a cab from the airport to your hotel, you will usually get there more quickly than waiting for the transfer vehicle whose fee might be included in a package deal. This is also true when returning to the airport for your flight home. The transfer vehicle usually calls for the return guests several hours before the flight is due to depart. That means sitting in the airport instead of on the beach or at pool side. Call a cab and plan to arrive at the airport one hour before departure time.

Use common sense when out and about in a new area. Keep all money and valuables locked up in the hotel safe when you are gone from your room. Always use traveler checks. Keep only the amount of money on your person that you plan to spend for a day. Petty thieves are on the lookout for unsuspecting people. Losing a small sum can be dealt with. Losing a large amount can spoil everything.

Don't over pack, especially if you are going to a warm climate. Tons of clothes are just not needed down near the equator. Several bathing suits will be more important than several dresses. If you can pack all into carry-on luggage, you will be better off. You can get through immigration quicker if you don't have to wait for luggage to be unloaded from the plane; and you will arrive at your hotel sooner.

Distant Wedding Organizer and Departure Checklist

Going away to be married can drastically reduce your need-to-do list, but even here you want to be sure that nothing is forgotten. A wedding organizer and departure checklist has been included on the following pages (see Figures 13.1 and 13.2). If your travel agent is going to assist with coordinating your away-from-home ceremony, she or he will also find the organizer a valuable planning tool.

Figure 13.1
Distant Wedding Organizer

Wedding Date _____   Desired Wedding Time _____

Type of Ceremony   ( ) Civil   ( ) Religious   Denomination _____

Setting for Ceremony   ( ) Church   ( ) Garden   ( ) Beach   ( ) Other

Wedding Budget $_____   Honeymoon Budget $ _____

Length of Stay for Wedding and Honeymoon _____

(Allow several days to fulfill residency requirements if needed)

Ceremony Requirements

( ) Bridal Bouquet   ( ) Groom's Boutonniere   ( ) Music   ( ) Video

( ) Wedding Cake   ( ) Photography   ( ) Champagne   ( ) Other

Special Request _____

Destination _____

Type of Accommodations   ( ) First Class   ( ) Beachside   ( ) Poolside

                             ( ) Superior   ( ) Gardenside   ( ) Other

Type of Cabin for Cruise Ship   ( ) Superior   ( ) First Class   ( ) Standard

Figure 13.2
Departure Checklist

Documents

       ( ) Passport

       ( ) Birth Certificates

       ( ) Photo I.D.'s

       ( ) Divorce Decrees (if applicable)

       ( ) Death Certificate of Previous Spouse (if applicable)

       ( ) Blood Tests

       ( ) Health Certificates

       ( ) Other Necessary Papers

Apparel

( ) Bridal Dress	( ) Tuxedo or Suit
( ) Headpiece	( ) Shirt
( ) Undergarments	( ) Underwear
( ) Jewelry	( ) Belt
( ) Shoes and Hose	( ) Shoes
( ) Purse	( ) Tie

Other

       ( ) Rings

       ( ) Camera

       ( ) Traveler's Checks

       ( ) Airplane Tickets—Airline _____

       ( ) Cruise Tickets-Cruiseline _____

       ( ) Miscellaneous _____

Hotel Name, Address, Telephone Number _____

Cruiseline Name, Address, Telephone Number _____

Name and Telephone Number of Contact Person for Wedding Service _____

❧ Selecting Your Travel Agent

"Fam trips" or familiarize trips, are made available to travel agencies by different locations and hotels to acquaint the agent with the accommodations, food, and entertainment of the various regions. Generally speaking, economics dictate that, more often than not, the owner or manager of the agency will take advantage of fam trips. Also, the owner or manager of an agency is more likely to network with other owners and managers. They can provide you with first hand information and more accurate knowledge of the destinations you might consider for your wedding and honeymoon. Contrary to this, the agency employees are frequently forced to rely heavily on brochures and the sales pitch of an area representative as selling tools. Brochures always portray inviting scenes, but do not always reflect reality. Empty pools, noisy rooms, poor food, and unsafe beaches are not uncommon complaints when trips are booked this way.

One of the major requirements of the place you select is that you absolutely do not want to be disappointed with it. Being married in a far-off location is different from simply vacationing there. Do not select anything budget. This is what you'll get, and you'll be disappointed. Budget accommodations are for college kids, not people about to cross this major threshold. Of course you have to work within your budget, but this is not really the time to skimp.

The destination you select should have things to do that interest both of you. You should be able to reach it without a lot of stress and fuss. Wherever you plan to stay, it should be safe, somewhat private, and beautiful. Seek out and settle for nothing less than first class arrangements and have a knowledgeable travel agent do your booking. If you are planning to be married and honeymoon far from home, you should be equipped to ask appropriate questions. Go to your selected travel agency prepared to do this. Without spending a lot of time and energy, you will begin to get a sense of the agent's knowledge and skill. If he or she can't answer all of your questions to your satisfaction, he or she should be able to access sources to get accurate information for you in a timely way. If a day or two passes and you do not have the necessary information or feel uncomfortable with the information provided, seek out another agency and try again. Like any business, some try harder and will do a much better job for you.

You need an agent that is savvy in his or her field and also well-traveled, for there are many choices in travel today. The agent's job is to get you the most up-to-date, accurate information, and help you to understand the destination you are considering. He or she should also be able to help you get the best value for your hard-earned dollars. If you both are new to international travel, you may want to pose some of these questions to your travel agent:

> *How populated is the area we plan to visit?*
>
> *If you plan to visit a far off location, how safe is it to wander about? Is there a lot of crime there?*
>
> *What is the literacy rate of its people?*
>
> *What are the people like?*
>
> *Is there a lot of poverty? How might this affect you if you plan to stay there?*
>
> *Have you gotten a lot of positive feedback from other clients that have visited there?*
>
> *Are there good travel connections for getting there?*
>
> *Are there any direct flights?*
>
> *How much of our time will be spent in travel getting to and returning from the area we are considering?*
>
> *What does a good meal cost there?*
>
> *Can we bring any food with us? Is there a small store near our accommodations where we can buy food and other things?*
>
> *If we are allowed to bring food, how do we transport it?*
>
> *What type of currency is used there? How does it compare to the dollar? Where is the best place to exchange our currency?*
>
> *What type of entertainment is available there?*
>
> *Is there a rainy season or hurricane season there?*
>
> *Will we need to rent a car to get out and about?*
>
> *Can we walk to most areas of interest?*
>
> *What is public transportation like there? What does it cost?*
>
> *What will a cab cost from the airport to our hotel?*
>
> *Is there an entry or departure tax?*
>
> *Have you ever been there?*
>
> *Could you connect us with someone who has been there?*
>
> *Have you ever done travel plans that relate to wedding plans?*

✦ The Reception/Celebration Party

The reception, designed to celebrate the new marriage, generally centers around a wedding feast with music and entertainment. The couple that chooses to marry away from home should also consider a celebration party on their return to their home community. With the wedding and honeymoon over, the bride and groom will be rested and somewhat comfortable with their new roles as husband and wife. They can look forward to the celebration knowing that nothing of great importance is apt to go wrong. They can anticipate a reception party where they too will enjoy the food and music along with their guests.

The reception following a distant wedding ceremony can be designed on all levels, from very informal to very formal, where the bride and groom wear their wedding attire once again. The couple's time, energy, and finances should guide them in planning the event. Generally, the reception is less formal than one of a traditional wedding. However, this is frequently balanced out by the couple receiving several reception parties in their honor, as they visit family and friends during their first year of marriage.

The away wedding is an option for many couples for many reasons. Here are a few final questions to ask yourselves to determine if this approach to matrimony might be right for you:

Do we desire a large crowd at our ceremony and reception?

Can we afford the traditional type of wedding?

Is a traditional type wedding important to either of us?

Are we the adventurous type?

Would any of our family or friends be able to come with us?

Is the ceremony and honeymoon more important to us than the frills that accompany the traditional wedding?

What time of year and planning time is most desirable and feasible for our wedding?

Is an "away wedding" an option for us?

Chapter Fourteen

Turning Fantasy into Reality

Weddings on the Move

❧ "The Train, The Train!"

If you have always had a love affair with trains, including a scenic train ride in your wedding ceremony is very possible. There are many old train lines that operate daily as scenic tours from one place to another and most of them are more than willing to assist you with the inclusion of your wedding ceremony at some point in their trip.

One of the most spectacular excursions in North America is the Agawa Canyon Train Tour. The tour begins in Sault Ste. Marie, just over the Michigan border in Ontario, Canada. The train winds its way some 165 miles north, "past the awesome granite rock formations of the Canadian Shield, through mixed forests of maple, birch and pine and alongside the pristine waters of northern lakes and rivers." From comfortable seats, through large picture windows, you can look out upon an unspoiled and rugged wilderness "that once was home to the Ojibway Indians, fur traders, lumberjacks and prospectors." The train also takes you across a train trestle 80 feet up in the air, and offers spectacular views of Lake Superior.

Within the last year or so, several couples have elected to hold their wedding ceremony in the beautiful Agawa Canyon, where the train has a two-hour stopover. There are many ways to set up a wedding ceremony that includes the train excursion to lead into your wedding ceremony and celebration party, for a large or small wedding ceremony. Getting an officiator to accompany the wedding party from Sault Ste. Marie down into the canyon is relatively easy. The following is an account of two different couples who chose to be married in this exciting way.

✒ Weddings that "Cake the Cake" and the Train

Donna and Kiley are two residents of Ontario, Canada, who were looking for a simple and memorable way to be married, when Donna's father, who works for the Algoma Central Railway, suggested a ceremony in the Agawa Canyon. Getting everyone to the wedding would include a three-hour scenic train ride into the beautiful canyon. Five-hundred-foot-high rock walls enclose the canyon, and there are several waterfalls that provide a natural and beautiful setting for a marriage ceremony. The two-hour stopover in the canyon allows plenty of time for a wedding and a picnic lunch.

> Kiley and I really wanted to just get married without a big fuss but my father wanted a wedding ceremony that included all our family and friends. He suggested that we rent two private cars for our immediate family and wedding party and take all of them and the rest of our invited guests by train, down into this beautiful canyon. He reasoned that this would be a lovely and very memorable place to be married. We would ride to our wedding site in "vintage" railroad cars, with red velvet chairs, rugs, and curtains. Our car would be at the very end of the long train, with large glass windows and a glass door, leading out onto the small platform, with a brass railing around it. It sounded very romantic to both of us and our families were happy when we consented to get married this way.

The couple, their families, wedding party, and over one hundred guests all boarded the train in Sault St. Marie for the three hour trip.

> We had a great train ride into the canyon. All of our immediate family and attendants rode with Kiley and me in the two vintage cars at the end of the train and the rest of our guests rode in the two train cars in front of us. The cost of the private cars included two meals, which we elected to use as a little buffet for all our invited guests. Everyone socialized with much fun and laughter during the train ride to and from the canyon, as they were able to wander back and forth into our private cars for a visit, good luck wishes, music, songs, and something to eat. When the train pulled into the Agawa Canyon, we all got off and assembled for the wedding ceremony. The park provided an especially scenic background with beautiful flowers, well-groomed lawns, and a special waterfalls named most appropriately "Bridal Veil Falls!"

It was a warm summer day and the weather couldn't have been better. Sunshine and soft breezes spilled into every corner of the exquisite park. I had a southern belle type of wedding dress and our attendants wore complementing attire. We used hoop skirts to go along with the train scene and parasols to keep the sun off our faces. The men in the party wore cut away tuxedos with top hats and canes. The entire scene resembled something from the turn of the century and the great "iron horse" that had brought us here seemed to authenticate it all.

The ceremony went off as planned and soon it was time for everyone to board the train again for their return trip to Sault Ste. Marie, where the couple had planned a celebration party at one of the many hotel sites available there.

Several of our attendants hung a "Just Married" sign off the brass railing on the little platform at the end of our car and this caused a lot of excitement on the train ride back to Sault Ste. Marie and also when we pulled into the station there. People stopped to look and wish us "good luck" all along the way. The train ride was so much fun for all of us and added a very romantic feeling and many special memories to our wedding ceremony. We were fortunate to have a day that was just about perfect in every way and were very happy that my father had guided us in this direction.

Betty and Russ, an older professional couple who lived in Madison, Wisconsin, also chose to be married in the fall of 1993 in Agawa Canyon. They had heard from friends about the wonderful train ride and the canyon's beauty and felt that it would provide a glorious and private place for them to be married. Unlike Donna and Kiley, they planned to have a very intimate and personal wedding day.

It was a second marriage for each of us and we didn't want a large crowd present. We contacted the people at the railway and asked for their assistance in providing two witnesses for our marriage ceremony. Russ's best man was actually one of the men who worked for the railroad and my maid of honor was a tour guide on the train, from Austin, Texas.

The couple had planned to be married at one of the waterfalls in the canyon, but as luck would have it, the day turned out to be cold and rainy. "The train ride and scenery was ever so beautiful, even in the rain. The fall colors seemed to take on a deeper tone and added a special brightness to our day."

When we arrived in the canyon, everyone was very supportive and helpful. It was suggested that we hold our marriage ceremony inside the cab of the great engine car, at the front of the train, because it was warm and cozy there. We climbed up several rungs of a ladder leading into this antique-looking, mighty engine car and assembled for our ceremony. There was the two of us, our minister, a photographer, a volunteer videographer, and our two witnesses. Together, we signed our marriage license here and were married in a 25-minute ceremony. It was very romantic and certainly different from the run-of-the-mill wedding ceremony. Following our marriage, we climbed down the 10-foot steel engine ladder and took our seats again on the train. As the long train pulled out of the station to head back to Sault Ste. Marie, the conductor announced that there had just been a wedding performed in the train's engine car and many, many people then made a point of coming up to our seats to speak with us and offer their congratulations. It was a very special beginning for us.

Betty and Russ encountered some difficulty securing their marriage license due to initial misdirection regarding Russ's divorce papers. However, with the aid of a fax machine, several friends back home, and the friendly and helpful guidance of a number of Canadians, they were able to secure their license and be married as planned in the canyon. "It was a second marriage for each of us and we encountered several unexpected snags in securing our marriage license due to corrective paperwork. In spite of this, everyone was very supportive and went the extra mile to help us so our marriage could take place pretty much as we had planned."

Several months after their memorable wedding, announcements were sent out and family and friends were all invited to a celebration party.

Russ designed a special announcement card with a train engine, replicas of our wedding rings, and railroad tracks with our names printed along them. We also carried the train theme into our wedding cake with a duplicate of our announcement card designed into the frosting. We had kept our marriage pretty much a surprise. No one knew really knew about it until they received our creative announcement card. It was a total surprise to all our family and most friends so we had much to talk about and celebrate at our party!

The cost of a train wedding, using the Agawa Canyon for the ceremony, will vary according to your ceremony and your needs. Vintage private cars seat from 8 to 12 people and food is included in the cost of the rentals. Trains run most of the year and there is even a "Snow Train" if you want a white wedding scene. Non-denominational ministers can be secured for your ceremony in Sault Ste. Marie and donations are usually made to their church in return for their accompanying you into the canyon and performing your ceremony. If you would like to further inquire about renting a vintage train car or planning a wedding ceremony in the Agawa Canyon, write or call

Algoma Central Railway, 129 Bay Street, Sault Ste. Marie 33, Ontario, Canada P6A 5P6, 1-705-946-7300.

Obtaining a license for a first marriage simply involves filling out application papers, which can be obtained through the mail. Appropriate identification papers must be presented and the application papers must be signed by both parties at the Civic Center in Sault Ste. Marie when you appear to pick up the license. There is then a three-day waiting period before the license can be used. The day the license is signed for and issued counts as day one. The license is valid for 90 days from the date it is issued. If one or more parties has been previously married, obtaining a marriage license is slightly more involved, but not impossible. An Ontario lawyer must be employed to review your divorce documents. The fee is nominal and both parties must appear at the lawyer's office to sign papers before the documents are sent off for approval from the main office that issues marriages licenses for weddings in Ontario. If the process is followed correctly, a license to marry can be obtained in approximately two weeks. The couple will be notified by mail that permission to marry has been granted and a license will be issued to them in Sault Ste. Marie upon their arrival.

The Civic Center operates from 8:30 a.m. to 4:00 p.m., Monday through Friday. (If you appear at 4 p.m. you can still obtain a marriage license if your application is in order, as the center actually closes at 4:30 p.m.) To further inquire about a marriage license for Ontario, Canada, write or call Civic Center, Office of Vital Statistics, Request for Marriage License, 99 Foster Drive, P.O. Box 580, Sault Ste. Marie, Ontario, Canada P6A 5N1, 1-705-759-5394.

❧ "Taking the A Train" in Scenic Vermont

Another great train that lends itself to weddings is available in Vermont. It winds its way along the hills and scenic valleys of the beautiful and quaint Green Mountain state, crossing a 90-foot gorge with a magnificent cascading waterfall, and passes several covered bridges and an old swimming hole along the way. The Green Mountain Flyer offers a twenty six mile scenic trip between Bellows Falls and Chester, Vermont, and many weddings have been performed both during the train ride itself and at stops along the way. The railroad operates from June through October and will soon expand its operating time into the cooler months.

The train makes a perfect location for a wedding with a western theme. "We recently did a rather large wedding of about 150 people. The entire wedding party and many of the guests were dressed in western style clothing. To go along with their western theme, they rented two of our classic wooden coaches, which were built in 1891 and are over a hundred years old. The marriage ceremony actually took place on the moving train."

The fall is a particularly beautiful time of year to arrange a train wedding in Vermont. Depending on the size of the party, several months advance notice may be required during this popular time of year. For smaller wedding parties and during the rest of the year, bookings should take place about two to three months in advance. Rates start at about $10 for a round trip ride. Wedding parties of all sizes are encouraged, from just the two of you to many invited quests if you desire. The cars will hold about 45 to 75 people, and group rates are available for 30 or more people.

Since Bellows Falls and Chester are located in two separate counties, a marriage license must be secured in the same county where the marriage is to take place, according to Vermont marriage license rules. If you plan your ceremony in Chester, or Windsor County, your license must be obtained there. If the ceremony is to take place along the way in Bellows Falls, or Windham County, the license must be secured there. There is no waiting period or blood test required in Vermont and the license is valid for 60 days from the date of issue. A referral list for obtaining a license and all desired services is available from the railroad. For more information, write or call Green Mountain Railroad Corp., Passenger Services, P.O. Box 498, Bellows Falls, Vermont 05101, 1-802-463-3069.

✎ "Up! Up! and Away in Our Beautiful Balloon!"

Your fantasy for a memorable wedding ceremony could include a magical flight, high above the earth in a colorful balloon and basket. A beautiful sky above your heads will forever be a vivid reminder of your special day. Many couples choose to be married in this way each year, and there are several experienced scenic balloon flight companies that can accommodate your desire to be married aloft.

One co-owner of Fantasy Balloon Flights, located in Thermal, California, told of a wedding that they once did for an octogenarian couple. "The couple held their wedding ceremony one thousand feet above the earth in our six-passenger balloon with their minister and wedding party aboard. What made their ceremony really unique was that thirty of their family members and friends also flew in hot air balloons along side them listening to their vows, via the aircraft radios."

Balloon weddings are dependent on weather conditions, so this has to be a consideration when planning a ceremony this way. If you are adamant about having a marriage ceremony aloft, being flexible with your wedding date and plans is recommended. Diana and Burton, a New Hampshire couple, wanted to have a very memorable wedding service when they won a balloon ride complete with a mini-celebration.

> It was a second marriage for both of us. Burt who was in his seventies was fighting cancer. This seemed a perfect way for us to be married as both of us were very adventurous people and we wanted to celebrate our marriage in a fashion that would be long remembered by all. However, the February day of our wedding turned out to be too windy to fly so rather than change our wedding date to another day, we elected to simply hold our ceremony, standing in the basket, on the ground. Several months later, when the weather permitted, we took our first balloon ride as Mr. and Mrs. to complete the ceremony. I have two sons from a former marriage and they were able to follow us across town in a friend's car by keeping our balloon in sight from the ground. The entire experience was very thrilling for all of us and I would highly recommend a marriage service this way if you are looking for something extremely memorable and not afraid of heights. It is very peaceful and at the same time exciting being aloft together this way, at this special junction in your lives. The blue sky above and a soft wind upon your face will forever hold marriage memories.

The cost of a balloon wedding service will depend on the rental fee in your area and the amount of time you wish to remain aloft. Rates range from $100-$150 per person, per hour. Most companies offer group rates. Some baskets will hold as many as nine people so you can plan to bring along a photographer, as well as the officiator and witnesses if you wish. For more information on this creative approach to marriage, two hot air balloon companies are listed following that have done many weddings aloft: Fantasy Balloon Flights, 83-701 Avenue 54, Thermal, California 92274, 1-800-462-2683 or 1-800-GO-ABOVE, and Unicorn Balloon of Colorado, 300 B Airport Business Center, Aspen, Colorado 81611 or 15001 North 74th Street, Scottsdale, Arizona 85260, 1-800-468-2477.

Chapter Fifteen

Mixing and Matching

Quick and Easy Ideas for Marriage Fun and Remembrance

Here are some quick and easy, fun things to do to make your wedding and future anniversaries exciting and memorable for yourselves, your families, and your guests. Most of these ideas will take only a few minutes of your time, and all of them will make your day even more special. Many of these ideas were used by brides and grooms searching for a way to make a personal statement about their wedding day to their family, friends, relatives, and each other.

☙ Prior to Your Big Day

1. *Make a special keepsake of your wedding invitation by mailing one to yourself. Do not open it. Keep it safely in your wedding guest book and save for future generations to open.*
2. *Listen to love songs before, during, and after working on your wedding plans. It will help you to stay focused on what marriage is all about as you set your plans in motion.*
3. *Select a special type of stamp to use for sending your invitation out. Ask for "Love" stamps or flower stamps to add feeling and color to the outside of your invitation as it arrives at the homes of your invited guests.*
4. *Cover an ordinary headband with some of the left over material from your wedding dress hem, to make a matching headpiece.*

5. Look for your cake knife at a yard sale. Buy a "one of a kind" knife and have it engraved with your names and wedding date. Decorate the handle with a colorful bow and streamers.

6. Fashion family flag-like banners, using your wedding colors and sparkle pens, with as many names, dates, places, and items of interest as possible, relating to each family history, and display them at the marriage ceremony and reception site.

7. Ask all relatives and guests to write a favorite recipe on the back of their response card and file these in a special recipe box to use during your married life.

8. Take ballroom dance lessons before your reception to look comfortable out on the dance floor and have more fun dancing at your wedding celebration.

9. Register for your gifts at the place where you need the most items, such as a hardware store, a sporting goods store, or a lumber yard if you are planning to build or remodel your home.

10. Shop at a pawn shop for something old to use in your ceremony.

11. Have stickers printed up with your names and marriage date and stick them on whatever type of original favor you may wish to give to your guests, such as homemade fudge, small bottles of champagne, jars of nuts, and so on.

12. Mix and match the types of flowers to be used for your arrangements. Use dried or silk flowers for the attendants and real ones for the bride and groom. This allows you to make, or to have made, a large portion of your floral arrangements long before your wedding day, if you are anxious to get things done ahead of time.

13. Write a love letter to each other on the evening before your wedding day and drop it in the mailbox on your way to your wedding ceremony. Save the letters for opening and reading on your first wedding anniversary.

14. Plan to use dried Hydrangea flowers, if they are available to you, for your attendants' floral arrangements. Pick them when they are in season and keep them in pitchers of water until they dry out and change color. Next remove them from the water and allow the stalks to dry completely. Fashion into arm-held bouquets and tie with colorful paper ribbon and store safely until your wedding day. Hydrangeas come in several sizes and colors, are easy to dry, and can be made into beautiful arrangements that will keep for several years after your wedding day.

15. Use readily available heart-shaped cookie cutters, jelling molds, and baking pans to make various types of desserts for your rehearsal dinner or reception party. Cookies, jelling salads, and ice cream cakes are a few ideas that will work well using this idea.

16. If you want to lose weight for your wedding day, take tap dancing lessons. It's fun, relaxing, and a great way to get into shape. You can even dance one of your numbers together to entertain your guests at the reception party.

17. Use your birthstone colors as your wedding colors to give additional meaning to your wedding scene.

18. Raise your own love seeds for throwing at your celebration party by planting sunflowers. Watching them grow will be a daily living and happy reminder of your approaching wedding day.

19. Include your zodiac signs as part of your wedding decorations on invitations, favors, the cake, napkins, and so on.

20. Incorporate the scene of the special place where you first met into your invitations, cake frosting, and all the decorations of your celebration party.

21. Have a fireworks display along with your rehearsal dinner.

22. The custom of engraving the inside of the wedding ring dates back to the time of Shakespeare, during the 16th century, and it was believed to give lasting meaning to the marriage ring. Some popular ring engravings of that period were:
    > "I will be yours while life endures."
    > "In thee my choice do I rejoice."
    > "God for me appointed thee."

    When you select your wedding rings, be sure to have them engraved with an endearing phrase or, more simply, the bride's name to his name on the groom's ring, and the groom's name to hers on the bride's ring, and the date of your marriage on each.

23. A very old Scandinavian custom said that the bride must make the groom's wedding shirt to insure a happy marriage. Make something for your groom to wear on his wedding day and bring happiness to your marriage too. (Use a piece of your wedding dress material and make him a wedding day bow tie!)

❧ The Day Itself

1. Have your attendants wear a "megatux." Place one half of a lottery ticket in a pocket of each of your attendants' tuxedos. Keep the other halves of the tickets in one of your own tuxedo pockets for good luck, and split the winnings with your groomsmen if one of the numbers comes up.

2. Dress your ring bearer in regular short pants, shirt, bow tie, and high top sneakers of a matching color. Use a pretty ribbon to tie a balloon of the same color to his ring pillow, for him to keep after he delivers the rings to you.

3. Always stand facing your assembly when you take your vows and speak up so that everyone present can hear clearly what you are saying. If the church is large, use wireless microphones to insure that your words can be heard by all your family and guests.

4. Sneak down to the marriage site early on your wedding morning to preview your flowers when they are set in place. Taking just a few private minutes to take this in before the ceremony will help you to remember how things actually looked at the place of your marriage, and you will feel less nervous as you enter the church or marriage place at the time of the ceremony.

5. Have your parents act as Matron of Honor and Best Man.

6. Hang colored balloons and ribbons on the lamp post, fence post, flag pole, or roof top of your home on the morning of your marriage to let the community and all your kindred spirits know that it is your wedding day. This also makes a nice reminder of the day's events when your family members and guests return home after the celebration.

7. Have a picture taken of the two of you standing in a field of dandelions, daisies, black-eyed Susans, bluebonnets, Indian paintbrush, or what ever wildflowers may be in bloom where and when your ceremony takes place. There is no greater decorator/designer than mother nature for a beautiful background to frame your first few moments of married life and wedded bliss.

8. Send flowers to the house of your soon to be husband's or wife's family on the morning of your wedding day. Sign with love and "soon to be your daughter-in-law" or "soon to be your son-in-law."

9. If your parents are divorced and remarried, create or have someone help you to create a poem about how each one of them relates to

your wedding day. Have your maid of honor and best man read your poetry at your marriage ceremony to build a bridge to better family understanding and support.

10. *It was an ancient Greek custom to give each bride and groom a branch of ivy as they stood before the temple to be married. The Ivy was a symbol of the indissoluble bond of matrimony." Give each other a sprig of ivy during your marriage ceremony and keep them side by side in a pretty pewter or crystal vase, some place visible in your home, as a reminder of this bond.*

11. *Hire a small private plane or helicopter and pilot to get from the church to the reception site, or to your honeymoon suite.*

12. *Other creative modes of transportation to and from the wedding site might be boat, bicycles, sleigh, stage coach, ferry boat, hot air balloon, snow shoes, skis, or a toboggan painted in your wedding colors.*

14. *Build your wedding plans around a club membership. Ride snowmobiles out to a beautiful overlook and hold your ceremony there. Hold a potluck celebration party afterwards.*

15. *If family or friends are shut-in or in the hospital on your wedding day, visit them in your wedding clothes. Bring them some of your wedding cake and flowers to help them celebrate your marriage too. Have a picture taken of the two of you at their bedside.*

16. *Release butterflies at your reception (call 1-800-334-5551 for more information), as a sign of the human metamorphosis brought about by love and marriage.*

17. *Dress up salt and pepper figurines as your cake top characters.*

18. *Release a pair of doves at your wedding reception as a symbol of the union of two living creatures, each with its own free spirits, yet mated for life.*

19. *Give jars of homemade preserves as favors. Fill small baby food jars with the preserves and cover with a piece of fabric and ribbon, using your wedding colors. Sign and date the top.*

20. *Give a piece of Swedish Ivy or a small spider plant to each guest as a living wedding favor from your home to theirs. Set the cuttings in small, used glass containers, covered in a pastel foil. Attach small cards with your names and wedding date to it by tying a wedding ribbon around the top of the container.*

21. *If you have a video made of the ceremony and reception, dedicate a song to all the relatives or friends that could not be present at your wedding. Actually read off their names so they will feel a part of the celebration when they get to view the video someday.*

22. In recognition of other married couples present at your celebration party, have a "for married couples only" dance. Give the DJ a list of all the couples attending your wedding and the number of years that they have been marries. As each couple's names are announced, along with the number of years of marriage they have celebrated, they can leave the dance floor until the last remaining couple, who have been married the longest, are out on the floor alone.

23. Give favors that are indicative of your hobbies. Some ideas might be golf balls and tees with your married names printed on them or key chains in the shape of your favorite pastime.

24. Avid hikers can prepare two hardwood walking sticks and have all your wedding guests sign their names on them using indelible ink or a sparkle pen, to wish you well in your journey through life together.

25. Wear two garters. Throw one and keep the other to pass down to future generations. Place a good luck charm on the garter and have each additional garter wearer do the same to increase good fortune for each successive family generation.

26. Enhance the crystal, silver, and white motif at a winter wedding celebration party by having an ice sculpture made. Make frozen centerpieces using jello molds in various shapes.

27. Hire an airplane to fly a "congratulations ——— and ———" sign over the site of your marriage ceremony.

28. If you are an avid collector, use your collection to enhance your celebration decorations. Use grandma's old linens on the tables, your glass dishes for floral centerpiece arrangements, or antique tools to hold some of your wedding flowers.

29. Have a special dance with all family and friends invited up onto the dance floor and use the music that was a favorite with each of your parents.

30. Release ladybugs at your ceremony or celebration party for good luck and happiness. Ladybugs are voracious eaters of aphids, which destroy plants. Legend has it that they were given their name after they saved a village from destruction by pests during the middle ages. Because of this, the colorful little cricket was named in honor of "Our Lady," the Virgin Mary, and have since been regarded as omens of good luck and happiness. For more information, call 1-800-289-6656.)

31. Give wildflower seeds as wedding favors. The beautiful wildflowers attract butterflies, which helps to pollinate plants. Ask your family and friends to scatter the seeds to make your wedding day a new

beginning for other plants and animals. Each spring, they will have a personal and beautiful reminder of your wedding day as the wild-flowers bloom and colorful butterflies come to feast and play among them.

32. Have swans at your marriage celebration. These beautiful creatures are legendary birds of Aphrodite or "Venus," the beautiful goddess of love.

33. It was once an old custom in Scotland for "bride's favors to be sewn all over the bridal gown," and then taken off the dress after the marriage by all attending the ceremony. This old custom could be reenacted to add some "hanky panky" humor to the party following the ceremony. Secure two small handkerchiefs, each with the initials of your best man and maid of honor, to the underside of your train or inside the bow on the back of your gown. Include a small ceremony during the celebration party where these honored attendants can remove the gifts you carry for them. You may want to sew a small piece of jewelry into each handkerchief as an added favor.

34. In the fifteenth century, before it became the custom to throw the bridal bouquet, "stocking throwing" was a popular way for the bride to pass on the good luck to others at the wedding. If you don't want to throw your bouquet, you can reintroduce this old tradition. Gather an old stocking and sock, tie a colorful ribbon to each, and together throw them to your family and guests for "good luck." If two people of the opposite sex catch them, form a large circle and invite them into its center for a dance known in the fifties as a "sock hop."

⤳ After the Wedding

1. Take some fresh flowers, the same as in your wedding bouquets, to a craftsperson after your wedding, and have a "wedding lamp shade" made for your home as a reminder of all the flowers at your wedding ceremony.

2. Buy a new silver dollar with your wedding year on it and add another one to your collection on each wedding anniversary.

3. Save an unopened bottle of champagne to be used for a toast on your twenty-fifth wedding anniversary or the "most special occasion" in your married lives.

4. Use some of the pretty wrapping paper that your shower and wedding gifts came in as a decorative border mat to frame wedding pictures.

5. Send your parents some flowers while on your honeymoon signed with love and your new married names.

6. Search out a new hobby or interest while on your honeymoon that you can always do together.

7. Start a perennial flower garden after your wedding day with one plant and add an additional plant each year on your wedding anniversary.

8. Make a donation to a needy school somewhere in your married names, to propagate knowledge and understanding and promote the message of love among all people. Celebrate your wedding anniversary by sending additional money each year to the personal and special fund you have created. Renew your wedding vows on your 25th anniversary in the schoolyard and plant a tree, one which is representative of the month in which you were married, there on that spot.

9. If rain is forecast for your wedding day, ask one of your attendants to save an empty wine bottle used for your wedding toast and have them collect some rain water and pour it into this bottle. Label the bottle with your new married names and the wedding date. Pack the bottle of rain water safely away and use it to christen your first child. In this way, even a rainy wedding day can be turned into something very special.

10. Remove two buttons from your wedding gown before it is packed away and have them made into a set of earrings that you can wear each wedding anniversary as a little reminder to both of you of your wedding day and wedding gown.

11. In addition to your marriage vows, make an additional vow to each other on your wedding night that you will always take some kind of family vacation each year to renew your sense of how lucky you are to have each other, no matter what your financial picture may be.

12. Play honeymoon whist throughout your marriage and have healthy rations of honeymoon salad ("Lettuce alone")!

⚘ "Hand Me Down" Customs

Many traditions used in modern-day wedding ceremonies are descended from a previous time, in one form or another. The customs of throwing flower petals, rice, wheat, or nuts, and the presence of small children in wedding ceremonies all come from ancient fertility rites that were practiced to encourage the procreation of future generations. Many of these customs were also intended to protect the bride and groom and add a measure of good luck and prosperity to their marriage and future family.

The following is a small collection of less widely recognized customs and traditions that you may want to reintroduce at your wedding for fun and for good luck. A few ideas for starting new traditions have also been added to this collection, to encourage you to think of a tradition of your own that could be instituted at your wedding and passed down at future weddings of family members or friends.

1. *Greek mythology has it that Prometheus, brother of Atlas, lit a torch from the sun and brought fire to earth to provide warmth and protection for mankind. Hold a giant bonfire celebration upon your engagement as a symbol of love, warmth, and protection you will extend toward each other in marriage and share it with your families and friends. (Collect paper and wooden litter from attics, cellars, and roadways to use as fuel for your fire and your engagement bonfire can be the start of a yearly ceremony to proclaim the same.*

2. *The knotted pretzel once was important in the royal wedding scene. In the 1600s it was used as a nuptial knot. It soon became a common occurrence at all weddings of that time for the couple to use the pretzel to wish on, like the modern day wishbone. This old custom can be easily reintroduced by setting out a pretzel for each couple on the reception tables. Attach colored ribbons and a note of instruction about the "wishing pretzels." Soon, all your guests will be making wedding wishes, using this ancient custom, for your success and happiness in marriage.*

3. *In Medieval times, a very common custom at weddings was a ceremony of actually "tying the knot." The knot was seen as "the symbol of indissoluble love, faith, and friendship." During the marriage ceremony, a short piece of rope was looped around the wrist of the bride and groom in a figure eight and tied into a knot at the center, between their two wrists. At the end of the ceremony, the loops of rope with*

the tied knot at its center were slipped off their wrists and retained as a reminder of their marriage commitment.

4. During the 1700s, it was a common custom for the single guests at the wedding to wrap a small piece of wedding cake in linen and pass it through the bride's wedding ring three times. The small piece of cake was then placed under the pillow at night, which was supposed to make that person dream of his or her future wife or husband.

5. In northern parts of Europe, an exchange of basil sprigs between two people in love was at one time symbolic of their faithfulness to each other.

6. It was once a tradition to bake a ring into the wedding cake. It was believed that who ever got the piece of cake with the ring in it would be the next to marry.

7. It was once custom for a bride coming from a family with little material wealth to give roses to her groom as a symbol of her love and worldly wealth.

8. An old German custom to insure that the couple would always belong to each other was enacted when the bride placed her foot on that of the groom's and when he knelt on a piece of her wedding dress some-time during the marriage ceremony.

9. An old European custom to insure a sweet marriage is to set sprigs of marjoram, the herb symbolizing sweetness, in your hope chest as you plan for your wedding day.

10. An old Scottish rite of betrothal was the licking of thumbs. If a woman accepted a man's proposal of marriage, they formally sealed the act by licking their right thumb and then pressing them together and vowing to be faithful to each other. Then they were formally engaged to be married.

11. During the 1600s rosemary was believed to be an "ensign of wisdom, love and loyalty" and was often carried in the bride's hands to the wedding altar. It was also tucked into the bridal bed to insure these qualities in a marriage.

12. An old custom in England at one time was to pour a pot of boiling water over the doorstep of the bride's home as she left for the church as a good luck charm for another woman. It was believed that another marriage would be proposed before the water had time to dry up, from luck passed on by the bride's footsteps touch-ing the doorstep. An old Slavic custom was for the mother of the bride to pour a glass of water over the step of the bride's new home

as a good luck token. People believed that this would help insure that the bride's new life would flow as smoothly as the water over the step.

13. An old Dutch custom to insure good luck in the marriage was for friends and relatives to throw flowers and evergreens on the doorway of a newly married couple.

14. A white rose was the sign of joy among Ancient Greeks. If you are of Greek descent, use white roses in your floral designs in honor of your ancestors and to insure joy in your marriage.

15. A very old wedding custom that is still used in the Jewish wedding ceremony of today, is the breaking of the glass. During the ceremony, the couple sips wine from the same glass, which is then smashed under the heel of the groom's foot. This symbolizes that they are joined in happiness and love for all eternity, as the splintered pieces of glass can never be put back together.

16. The orange blossom has been used in weddings since very early times because it was believed to bring good luck and happiness to the marriage. Legend has it that "Jupiter was given an orange by Juno as a gift on their wedding day."

17. It is an old Scottish custom for the groom to give his bride a silver spoon as a wedding gift, symbolizing that they will never be hungry.

18. It is an old Irish custom for the groom to give his bride a silver coin during the marriage ceremony as a symbol of all his worldly worth.

19. Prior to having a wedding cake at the wedding celebration, it was the custom for the wedding guests to bring spice buns to the wedding celebration and stack them up on a table or plate before the bride and groom. Legend has it that "if the couple could exchange a kiss over the piled high stack of buns without disturbing them, they would enjoy lifelong prosperity."

20. An old custom to insure happiness for the bride is for her to step over the door sill of the church with her right foot as she enters it for the marriage ceremony.

21. Myrtle was used in ancient times at weddings because it was believed that it was a symbol of unfailing duty and affection.

22. During Anglo-Saxon times of the 13th and 14th centuries, brides gave knotted ribbons to friends to wear or carry at their wedding ceremonies. The knot served as s symbol of indissoluble love and duty.

23. Among the Navaho Indians, it was once a tradition for the man and woman to eat a bowl of corn pudding together as a way of solemnizing their marriage.
24. The custom of having a flower girl at the wedding dates back to the Middle Ages. It was believed that having flower girls in the ceremony would bring happiness to the marriage. They were given rose petals to strew on the bride's path to her groom as another way of insuring good luck for the couple in marriage.

❧ Fanciful Ideas

1. Give your love a twinkling star as a wedding gift. The international star registry will provide you with telescopic coordinates for a star that is copyrighted in your name, for a fee of $40.00. For more information, call 1-800-282-3333.
2. Keep a small piece of all clothing and paper material from your wedding reception, and honeymoon. Make a collage for framing and name it "GuessWhat!"
3. Give each other a "surprise" wedding gift. (Something other than the honeymoon trip or you could both be going in separate directions!)
4. Hire a skilled craftsperson to make you a quilted picture for your home, using pieces of fabric from your wedding dress, bridesmaids' dresses, mothers' dresses, and flowergirl's dress. A pattern known as the Dresden Heart Design uses sixteen wedge shapes of material, quilted together. The end product is a beautiful piece of artwork to decorate a wall in your home and a living, vivid reminder of the various wedding apparel worn in your wedding ceremony.
5. If you have children from a previous marriage give them a special gift from you and your new spouse. It can be something as elaborate as a piece of engraved jewelry or something as simple as a letter or poem that you have written together to express your love and future hope and plans for your newly formed family.
6. Different types of herbs are thought to be symbolic of certain traits and emotions. Add a little magic to your marriage through your floral

*arrangements by including one or more of the following herbs,
because of their "special powers."*

Thyme	Courage
Sage	Immortality
Rosemary	Love
Parsley	New Beginnings
Lion's Tail	Good Cheer
Marjoram	Sweetness
Hawthorne	Hope
Basil	Faithfulness
White Willow	Joy
Bay Laurel	Glory
Clover	Kindness
Ginger	Strength

7. *Make your first holidays together very special in some imaginative way. Always remember each other on Valentine's Day. The vestiges of this romantic tradition date back more than one thousand years. (There must be something to it!)*
8. *Build a "newlywed" bird house. The occupants will return year after year to nest and sing to you of your wedding day.*
9. *If two households are coming together and have two of most things, ask your wedding guests to make a donation in your new married names to your favorite charity or cause, instead of buying you another gift that you really don't need.*
10. *Make a Christmas tree ornament from the wine cork on the bottle of champagne used for your wedding toast, to recall wedding day memories each holiday season. Make several other ornaments using the corks from other toasting bottles and give one to each of your married children one day for their Christmas tree decorations.*
11. *Start your wedding album off with pictures from your babyhoods, childhoods, dating years, and finally the wedding day celebration photos.*
12. *Pass on some wedding magic. Build a "wedding" bench and carve your names and wedding date into the back of it and donate it to your favorite town park so that other couples may sit to communicate in a beautiful and tranquil place. Invite others to carve their initials and wedding date into the bench for good luck.*

13. Propagate the ivy vines form your bouquets to use as keepsake house plants. Use the same ivy plant in your children's bouquets when they get married.

14. Give your new bride or groom something that you can add on to with each wedding anniversary: a cultured pearl or semi-precious stone that can one day be made into a bracelet or necklace, a leather bound book of one of the classics that can be the beginning of a beautiful, personal library, something very special that is symbolic of your love and commitment to each other, or perhaps just a simple rose that will multiply into several dozen as the years pass.

15. Down through the ages, flowers have given different meanings to the wedding bouquets and wedding decorations. You may want to weave different flowers into your wedding day because of the meaning associated with them.

Apple Blossoms	Hope, awakening
Carnation	Love, promise, beauty
Chrysanthemum	Wealth, abundance
Clover	Hope
Daisy	Innocence
Forget-me-not	Remembrance, true love
Fuschia	Humble love
Hazel	Peace, reconciliation
Heliotrope	Undying devotion
Holly	Friendship, happiness
Ivy	Friendship
Jonquil	Desire
Lily-of-the-valley	Happiness
Locust	Eternal love
Mimosa	Sensitivity
Mistletoe	Perseverance
Pansy	Tenderness, thoughtfulness
Red Tulip	Passion
Rose	Love, grace, beauty
Wallflower	Fidelity, sincerity

16. Give each other a unicorn as a wedding gift. The legendary unicorn was a symbol of the power of love. Spread the power of love by giving a unicorn as a wedding gift to each wedding you attend thereafter.

17. Celebrate nature as newlyweds by making a small donation in your married names to the National Wildlife Federation to help other animals and plants procreate and replenish the earth. For more information, call 1-800-732-6564. Donations can be made in amounts of five dollars and up.

18. Begin a new tradition by placing a new penny inside your wedding album for each year of marriage. This will bring back wedding day memories on each anniversary as the album is taken off the shelf and opened to insert another penny

19. Continually cultivate your love by always starting and ending each day with a loving word or caress from your wedding day onward.

Chapter Sixteen

Turning a Sow's Ear into a Silk Purse

Minimizing Problems and Addressing Crisis Situations

Sometimes life's plans can cause wedding plans to go amiss. When this happens it becomes necessary to be able to graciously pick up the pieces, artfully rearrange them, and get on with the show. This can mean changing one or many parts of your original plan. One wonderful true life story can best demonstrate how this can happen and what others have done to cope with a difficult situation and still have a beautiful and memorable wedding celebration.

One bride and groom planned a very large wedding with a great number of invited guests. The bride's mother herself was a wedding consultant and had helped plan many large and beautiful weddings. Her daughter's wedding was to have over 250 invited guests and be a formal affair. The wedding dress and attendants' gowns had been bought and everything else set into place. Things seemed on course. Shortly before the invitations were due to go out what seemed like a catastrophe hit the family. With little or no warning, fickle fate waved its hand at the family as the bride's father, through no fault of his own, lost his job. Life had thrown this family a very serious curve. The funds, so generously planned for the wedding, suddenly became the object of silent focus.

Neither parent wanted to disappoint their daughter so nothing was said as they determined to press on. The father had worked for the same company for many years. "It was a very difficult thing for us to cope with. He was offered several other jobs so it wasn't like we were going to go hungry but it was a serious blow to our esteem. It was, to say the least, a very difficult period in our life at the wrong time." He quietly worried about his and his family's future. The mother quietly worried about her husband's self-esteem and how they could financially and emotionally deal with such a large wedding at this point in time.

A week or so after this family crisis, the mother received a phone call one morning from her daughter.

> She said that she and John had been thinking about their wedding and had decided that they wanted to rearrange things somewhat. They both felt that a big wedding was wrong at this point in time for them and their families. She was the child we had both raised. Very sensitive to the needs of her parents and family.

> Instead of being married in the big church with the expensive country club reception that had been originally planned, we talked about their being married at our home and having the reception here also. The more we discussed it the better it felt for all of us. This meant however making many changes. For starters, we had to cut the guest list from 250 down to about 90. Then there was the bridal dress that had a cathedral train. Neither of us felt it would go in the backyard, so that too would have to be cut. In spite of all the drastic changes we were facing, we all felt instant relief and the new wedding plan generated great excitement, happiness, and activity once again in our household.

Turning a wedding plan about is easy to do when your heart is in it. The cathedral train of the bridal gown was completely cut off and the garment was made into a tea length dress to make it fit in with a home wedding and outdoor reception. "We used the lace from the train to make a matching hat for my daughter's new wedding dress. It was absolutely beautiful and she never looked or felt lovelier. The leftover material was also used to fashion other accessories for the wedding.

"The guest list was cut down to include only the immediate family and a few very close friends that knew our children well." Everything from the size of the cake to the reception menu was changed to fit their new theme of a home wedding and reception. "The big wedding we had originally planned was just the wrong event for the wrong time so we redesigned it to make it work for us. This meant that we all had to think in a different direction from the original plan and be very open to suggestions."

The father was assigned the job of sprucing up the yard so that it would look presentable on his daughter's wedding day.

> This was very therapeutic for him because it gave him something to occupy his time. It also gave him the time and energy he needed to begin to think through what he wanted to do about a new job, once the wedding was over. In the process, the yard never looked so beautiful! All the shrubs got a trimming and the rose gardens were pruned and became very vivid and prolific once again. Dad edged all the flower gardens and bordered them with pink geraniums to match the pink table cloths we planned on using. We all pulled together and felt good again about this wonderful event. Instead of being a stressful time, it became a very dear and happy time in all our lives. We were all very flexible because each of us truly wanted to make each other happy for this most joyous day. A wedding is so much more that just a big party. The ceremony itself is what is really important and perhaps where most if not all of the emphasis should be focused.

The wedding day was wonderful because everything about the family and their home seemed to have a special glow to it.

> It was truly one of the most beautiful weddings I had ever been involved with in spite of having to change everything around. Everything just seemed to smile on us that day because this wedding had a very special tone to it that all the money in the world could not have provided. It was a time of great joy and love for our family and close friends. Adversity can always be turned into advantage even when it involves a wedding catastrophe of some kind.

❧ An Ounce of Prevention . . .

Much time and energy will be required to get you to this very special day in your lives. Planning a wedding can also become a stressful and worrying time. To prevent problems from occurring and minimize those that do, consider the following menu of things to keep the process of planning your wedding fun and make your wedding day more joyful.

Make a realistic wedding plan to begin with. Design a day that will allow you to reach your goal of marriage, without undue stress and complications. Plan according to your identities, time frames, and financial means.

Be organized and disciplined. Staying focused prevents needless spinning of wheels and wasting of time, energy, and resources.

Allocate enough time to activate and complete your preparations. Whether you buy or make the supporting structures of your wedding plan, whether your wedding is big or small, allow yourselves enough time to complete the task at hand.

Pay attention to details. Little things make up the whole of anything. Paying attention to small points of your plan can prevent big problems and headaches from occurring down the road. Little meaningful things will be long remembered by you and all your guests.

Keep a positive attitude. Keep the reasons why you are getting married in clear focus. Everything else should take a back seat to this.

Make decisions. Regardless of the size of your wedding, big or small, the merging of two lives will require many decisions. Like anything else, your gut instinct is usually the best indicator to help you to decide on important wedding issues and items. Rely on it.

Make changes. Be prepared for Murphy's Law and make detours when needed. When something goes amiss, view it as a creative challenge to redesign or rearrange the problem into something even more interesting and beautiful than it was previously.

Finalize things. Completing the different parts of your plan will prevent loose ends from distracting you as you move your attention onward.

Get each other's input. Two people are getting married. Two heads and four hands will lighten the load. Take an active part in planning your wedding, be you bride or groom.

❦ Building Bridges with Uncooperative Family Members

If either you or your spouse-to-be come from a mixed or broken family and there are damaged or hurt feelings among parents, it can be more than difficult to try to get them all together for your wedding day. Some couples end up feeling like they are entering a minefield. Trying to sort out which extended family members to invite and how to arrange seating among enemies can also seem impossible. There is no easy answer to all of this. You will not be able to mend torn fences because they are not yours to mend. The best thing is simply to say to each "combatant" that you understand that they may harbor less than friendly feelings for others invited to your wedding, but that you love them all and want all of them present to witness your special day. Ask them to call an eight-hour truce for your wedding day and leave it at that. If a loved parent or relative refuses to come, or remains difficult to deal with, keep his or her behavior in perspective and get on with your plans. It is your day to be joyful. If family members choose to mope or be spiteful or even stupid about your wedding plans, this is their problem, not yours. If you have a video made, blow a special kiss to each of them, the happy ones and the unhappy ones, the ones that were there and the ones that chose not to attend, and tell them that you love them all so that they will exist on your wedding film, if only in memory, in a combined friendly spirit at your wedding celebration. Send the ones who could not or would not attend a copy and get on with your wonderful new lives together.

◆ Ten Salvaging Techniques

Have an emergency kit on hand. Always prepare a small emergency clothing repair kit. Include some thread of the various colors of the different wedding apparel to be used in your wedding ceremony. Also include several pins of various sizes, small scissors, and a few paper clips. If something accidentally gets torn or needs to be reinforced, you are prepared. Brides often tell stories after the wedding about "Uncle Harry" unknowingly stepping on her train and having it rip out of the dress. One told of leaning over to kiss a relative during the receiving line and "he unknowingly stepped on the front of my gown. When I stood up straight again, the entire front of my dress ripped out. There I stood with a gaping hole in my beautiful dress." A quick repair job was done with the little emergency kit her mother had on hand and the party continued. These things do happen. Don't let them spoil things. Let only joyful tears fall on this special day.

Have an auxiliary plan available. Try to spend a little time anticipating what could go amiss with your wedding plan and map out an "alternate route," or a plan B and plan C, for each part of your original plan. If someone suddenly drops out of the wedding party, who could slip into the dress or tuxedo and take up the slack? Do you really need to have the same number of female and male attendants if this happens? (Asymmetrical can be just as beautiful as symmetrical. Think of the stars in the heavens or an arrangement of flowers. The more variance the more interest and beauty to behold.)

Make your family and attendants aware of the flow and their specific job. Provide them with a simple, handwritten schedule of events so everyone is cued in and using the same plan and time frames. Inform all persons about the things that you specifically need and what they will be responsible for, like this:

Our schedule of wedding day events is as follows:

1. _____
2. _____
3. _____
4. _____
5. _____

Roses are red,
Violets are blue.
Frank, these are the things
We especially need you to do:

l. A reading at our ceremony using a poem about love and marriage. Can be an "original" or one that you search out or one that you already know and love.
2. Distribute the payment envelopes to everyone as marked on the front of the envelope during our wedding day, i.e., minister, organist, etc. (Dick will give you the envelopes at our rehearsal dinner.)

Thanks for your help,
Sandy and Dick

Try to secure an alternate inside space if you are planning an outdoor ceremony. The ceremony and party can continue in warmth and coziness if the weather does not cooperate with your outdoor theme. One couple rented a tent for their reception. It was carefully laid out on the lawn, ready to be raised on the day before the wedding. Because of extremely heavy rain that night, the owner was unable to raise the tent as planned on the day before the wedding.

The tent looked like a large swimming pool lying there on the ground. Everything was soaked and it was still raining hard that morning with the forecast calling for even heavier rain on our wedding day. Because our home was very small, we decided to call around to different restaurants to see if we could find an establishment that normally did not do weddings and rent it for a few hours. Ours was a June wedding so we knew that everything else was already booked. After several calls, we found an owner that agreed to close his doors to the public for five hours on the following morning so we would have a warm place to eat, dance, and be merry. It was small and a little crowded but warm and cozy inside as the wind and rain howled outside. It worked out just fine.

Imagine what you would dress in if something happened to your wedding apparel. On occasion, the dress of your dreams may not work out for reasons beyond your control, and this can be a devastating blow. Is there another dress in the background someplace that you could use? One bride told of how when she went to pick up her wedding gown the Monday before the wedding, the seamstress had ruined it doing the alterations.

> Even my father who knows nothing about sewing recognized the mess the garment was in. My mother's dress was quickly retrieved from the attic and that is what I was married in. At first I was very sad but I determined to not let a dress spoil our marriage. A wedding dress is expendable. Our marriage would be everlasting. In an unexpected way, wearing my mother's wedding dress made our ceremony more special.

You'll be just as married regardless of what you wear, so don't let a piece of cloth spoil your day. Above all else, make it a happy and wonderful day.

Remember that everything can be fixed in some way. The old adage "adversity is the mother of invention" is sometimes very appropriate for wedding scenes. Something usually goes wrong at some point in the total process. Use your head and imagination to fix it. Make it even better than the original plan. If something is forgotten or overlooked, don't tell anyone and no one will know that something is missing. At my wedding, my going-away corsage never reached the reception site. It was left in a box at the back of the church. My maid of honor quickly fashioned a mini-corsage for me out of my bridal bouquet. No one was ever the wiser and someone back at the church had a lovely orchid to wear to mass the following day. I was very young, just 22, and felt a little sad because this had happened. I have since come to fully understand that everything can be fixed in some way to make it work. (Death is the only thing in life that is irreversible!)

Remember your family and guests. It is your day but some special consideration for your family and guests, who may have traveled far and given up of their time to be with you, will make your party more loving and fun for you. In the beautiful poem "Song of Hiawatha," Longfellow tells how at the wedding feast "the gracious Hiawatha, And the lovely Laughing Water, And the careful old Nokomis, Tasted not the food before them, Only waited on the others" (Longfellow, p. 191).

Start your plans off on the right foot. If something doesn't feel just right, pay attention to your instincts. They seldom will fail you. Make a wedding plan and wedding day that is yours not someone else's. Don't worry about what someone will think or say, only about what you feel in your hearts is right for the two of you.

Keep a small make up kit with a few essentials in it handy at your celebration party to insure a radiant glow throughout the day.

When all else fails, whistle. Courage to follow your convictions in the face of adversity is sometimes difficult to summon up. Practice whistling a little tune now and then to give yourselves a boost when and if things become difficult with your wedding plans and maintain your course. Above all else, on that special morning, Be Happy; It's Your Wedding Day!

Chapter Seventeen

"Extra, Extra, Read All About It!"

Creating Your Newspaper Byline

Your wedding has passed and now it is time to roll the presses and sum up the particulars of your wedding party and the fashions that were worn. Understanding a little designer language will help you to create just the right words to accompany your local newspaper photograph and inform the community of not only what transpired, but also how everyone was dressed for your big day. The information you give to the press should be detail-descriptive, vivid, and short. The following will help you to pull your apparel descriptions easily together. The jargon can be used to describe all types of apparel, whether your ceremony was traditional or not.

✎ Materials

Satin—smooth fabric with very shiny finish; comes in many different colors and shades of white and ivory, and in different weights

Taffeta—a silk imitation fabric; comes in different colors and different weights; finish is dull and can be either smooth or have a file-like appearance.

Silk—smooth, softer than taffeta, natural fiber; dull finish with different weights and colors; "natural silk" color is usually more off-white than white.

Tulle—sheer netting-like material. Used for dresses and veils.

Shantung—a heavy, silk-like material made from rayon or cotton; finish is silk-like in appearance with a ribbed effect.

Brocade—a heavy fabric with a design woven into it. Finish can be shiny or dull; often made of cotton blends.

Charmeuse—very soft and drapable, silk-like material with a semi-shiny finish.

Crepe—light weight, thin fabric with a sponge like finish.

Cotton Blends—natural fibers usually blended with polyester; finish is usually dull but can be semi-shiny when "polished."

Moire Taffeta—silk or synthetic fabric, characterized by a wavy water-like marking.

Georgette—thin, crepe-type material with a dull finish.

Organza—a synthetic fabric with a sheer and silky look.

Eyelet—fabric with embroidery-trimmed holes that make up a pattern.

✎ Dress Descriptions

Princess Line—dress designed with smooth, shoulder-to-hem unbroken lines. Front bodice and skirt are usually cut in three, full, long pieces of material without interruption at the waist. Skirt flares slightly.

Empire—A neoclassic French dress design that features a very high waistline, directly below the bust, a straight or slightly gathered, loose skirt.

Sheath—a gown that is fitted and has a straight skirt.

A Line—dress cut in several panels that go from top to bottom without an interruption at the waistline; slightly less flared at the hemline than a princess style.

Princess Line   Empire   Sheath   A Line

∿ *Necklines*

Bateau—*a boat-shaped neck using a straight or semi curved line from shoulder to shoulder.*

Cameo—*indicative of a decorative cameo image motif at the center front; cameo netting motifs are also used to embellish trains of wedding dresses.*

Jewel—*a circle around the natural neckline.*

Portrait—*neckline characterized by a large "V," to give emphasis to the face and shoulders.*

Queen Ann—*sculptured neckline, high in the back and sides and open in the front of the bodice, with a heart-shaped line across the top of the bust.*

Queen Elizabeth—*characterized by a back stand-up collar that sweeps around into a V shape at the front of the bodice.*

Sabrina—*similar to Bateau, but starts about two inches inside the shoulders and goes straight across; frequently has lace trim.*

V-Neck—*a V-shaped neck that begins at the base of the natural neckline in back and sweeps into a narrow V in the front of the bodice.*

Scoop—*round and low neckline at the front of the bodice.*

Sweetheart—*open neck with a heart-shaped line across the top of the bust.*

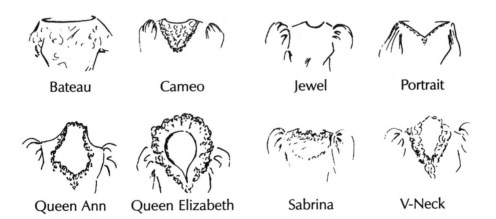

Bateau   Cameo   Jewel   Portrait

Queen Ann   Queen Elizabeth   Sabrina   V-Neck

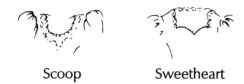

Scoop   Sweetheart

ᴥ Skirts and Waistlines

Bouffant—dress with a very full skirt.

Bubble—skirt is full and pulled up under at the hemline by attaching the full outer skirt hem to a shorter, less full lining. Comes in various lengths.

Gathered—dress gathers at the waistline are looser and material falls more softly than a full skirt design.

Tiered skirt—skirt formed with several graduated layers.

Mermaid skirt—skirt that is flared at or below the knees.

Antibellum waist—"natural" waistline that drops into a point at the front bodice by two or more inches.

Asymmetrical waist—waist design that starts out at the "natural" waist and then drops off dramatically to one side.

Dropped asymmetrical waist—same as above except entire waistline is dropped. Starts off below natural waist and continues in an asymmetrical line.

Basque waist—waistline that is dropped about two inches below the "natural" waistline and comes to a point in the front of the bodice.

Natural waistline—top and bottom of the dress are attached together in a straight line that goes across at the "natural" waist, about two inches above the hips.

Dropped waistline—top and bottom of garment attached together with a straight waistline but entire line is dropped below the "natural" waist by several inches.

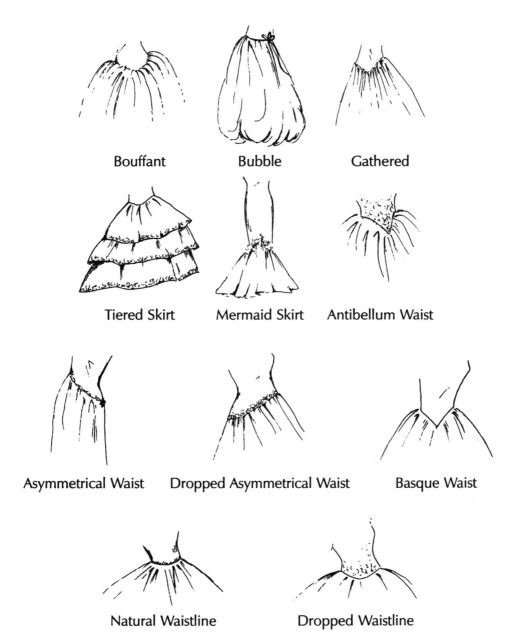

Bouffant   Bubble   Gathered

Tiered Skirt   Mermaid Skirt   Antibellum Waist

Asymmetrical Waist   Dropped Asymmetrical Waist   Basque Waist

Natural Waistline   Dropped Waistline

ᴥ Sleeves

Bow—off-the-shoulder sleeve characterized by a semi-large bow as the focal point of the sleeve.
Bell—flared sleeve that can be short or full length to the wrist.
Bishop—sleeve that is full and gathered into a cuff at the wrist.
Cap—short, fitted sleeve that covers just the very upper arm.
Capelet—sleeve that is softly flared; falls almost to the elbow.
Fitted—usually full-length sleeve that hugs the arm like a glove.
Puffed—fully gathered, short sleeve, worn off or on the shoulder.
Leg-of-Mutton—long fitted sleeve with a very full puff at the top.
Gibson—like a Leg-of-Mutton, but the puff is less full and it gathers more softly into a long fitted sleeve at the wrist.
Poet—very full, pleated sleeve, gathered into a large cuff.
Petal—short, full sleeve with several layered panels.

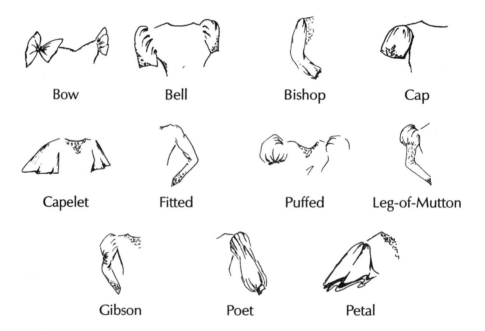

| Bow | Bell | Bishop | Cap |

| Capelet | Fitted | Puffed | Leg-of-Mutton |

| Gibson | Poet | Petal |

∾ Hemlines

Ballerina—bottom of hem comes to the top of the ankles.
Ankle length—bottom of hem reveals only a hint of the ankle.
Floorlength—bottom of hem falls one-half to one-and-a-half inches above the floor.
Street length—bottom of hem falls to the mid-knee.
Tea length—bottom of hem fall to the mid-calf.
High/Low—hemline is shorter in the front than the back. Can be done in various combinations of lengths.
Mini—hemline falls to above the knee.
Handkerchief—uneven hemline that is cut with several long, pointed edges; resembles a hanky that is peeking out of a breast pocket.

∾ Trains

Detachable—one that buttons or hooks onto the dress back.
Royal—train that extends beyond the waist by more than three yards.
Cathedral—train that extends from the waist three or more yards in length.
Chapel—one that extends from the waist one-and-a-half yards in length.
Semi-cathedral—train that is somewhere between the length of cathedral and chapel.
Sweep—short train that extends beyond the bottom dress hem by several inches and "sweeps" the floor.
Brush—very short train that just barely "brushes" the floor.
Watteau—train that is attached at the shoulders of the dress.

∾ Details and Embellishments

Applique—lace or fabric cut-out that is sewed onto a main piece of fabric, such as the bodice, sleeve, skirt, or train.
Bertha collar—wide lace or fabric trim around the top of a dress worn on or off the shoulders.
Bustle—large gathering of fabric pulled up into the back of the dress.

Panniers—large gathers of material attached to the waistline and draped over the hips.

Wedding band collar—high neck, stand-up collar that encircles the neck and may be trimmed with lace, beading, and sequins.

Yoke—broad piece of material that fits across the shoulders or across the hips to join up with the bodice or skirt.

Apron—long overskirt frequently trimmed with lace.

Keyhole—opening of various shapes used in the front and back of dresses.

Peplum—short flounce or overskirt of various cuts of material that encircles the waist.

Butterfly—large embellishment attached to the back of the dress that drapes downward.

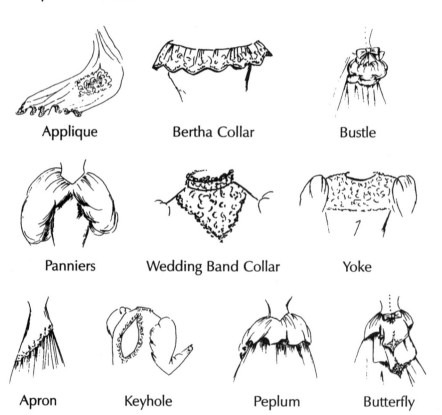

Applique   Bertha Collar   Bustle

Panniers   Wedding Band Collar   Yoke

Apron   Keyhole   Peplum   Butterfly

❧ Types of Lace

Chantilly—light-weight, crisp-feeling, inexpensive lace with a net backing.
Venise—heavy lace with no net backing; a free-standing lace.
Alencon—heavier-type lace with a pattern that has been re-embroidered with a heavy thread; pattern has a net backing; the most expensive lace.
Schiffli—the most delicate lace; a fine lace similar to Chantilly, but has less body and a finer net backing; the stitch used to form the lace has a satin quality and look to it.
Battenburg—country lace; a band of ribbon that is folded and manipulated into various shapes and then stitched together into a pattern; no net backing.

❧ Veil Description

Shoulder length—24 inches in length.
Chest length—29 inches in length.
Elbow length—35 inches in length.
Finger tip length—42 inches in length.
Walking length—52 inches in length.
Chapel length—88 inches in length.
Cathedral length—106 inches in length.

❧ Types of Veiling

Poly Illusion—synthetic netting
English Silk—silk netting
Sparkle Illusion—synthetic netting that has a shine and catches the light.
Blusher—short veil that comes down over the face

✒ Types of Headpieces

Juliet Cap—small fitted cap that sits over the crown of the head.

Tiara—crown that can be made of jewels, lace, flowers, or a combination of all of these.

Wreath of Flowers—circle of real, silk, or dried flowers.

Bandeau—band of flowers that extends from ear to ear.

Asymmetrical bandeau—band of flowers that starts above one ear and extends down over the other.

Halo or "V"—circle or V-shaped band that encircles the forehead.

Headband—decorative rigid band extending from ear to ear.

Hats—various styles from Derby to Picture hat with different types of flowers and beading details; sometimes referred to as a large or small "wedding hat."

Combs—ribbons, bows, or flowers of various colors.

Beading—seed pearls, pearls, sequins, or crystal.

✒ Creating Your Byline

Picking and choosing the correct description for your wedding apparel from the above, your local news byline might be created to read as follows:

The bride/bridesmaids/mothers/flower girl wore a
Color of dress _____
Type of material _____
Length of dress _____
Style of dress _____

The dress featured a
Type of neckline _____
Type of collar _____
Type of waistline _____
Type of skirt _____
Type of sleeve _____
Type/length of train _____

The dress was embellished with
Type of lace _____
Type of detail _____

The bridal headpiece was
Type of headpiece _____

The bridal veil (if one was worn) was
Color of veil _____
Type of veil _____
Length of veil _____

The bridesmaids/flowergirls wore headpieces of . . .
Type/color of flowers _____
Type of hats _____
Type/color of ribbons _____
Type/color of combs _____

Chapter Eighteen

Creating "Magic Moments, Filled with Love"

Keeping Romance Alive

When you set out to begin your plans for your wedding day, put your honeymoon near the top of the list of things to organize. Couples sometimes make the mistake of not looking into a honeymoon trip at the onset of their wedding preparations and as a result, often run short of funds by the time they start to focus on this part of their wedding plan. When this occurs, you run the risk of a shortened or "delayed honeymoon" or no honeymoon at all. I often have heard couples say, "we're going to take our honeymoon next summer, when we both have vacation time." Vacation and honeymoon are two different things. Vacations are wonderful but the period immediately following your marriage is a time unlike any other. Recognize it as a unique and special period, deserving of time off from the mundane affairs of daily living.

Other couples may think, because they have lived together for a time before their marriage, that a honeymoon is frivolous and unnecessary.

Marriage is different from merely living together. It is a new and different way of looking at life, an entirely new direction for both of you. The time spent together during the honeymoon period is an exercise in bonding as a married couple, before you reenter the pond of daily activities and responsibilities. Honeymoon time isn't merely the decoration on the marriage cake; it is one of the important ingredients of your marriage, that being time alone for each other. This period of time can set the tone for many happy and joyful years of married life to come. Make your honeymoon plans as important as your wedding plans and you will be starting your marriage off on the right foot.

◆ Taking the Time to Begin Anew

After the marriage ceremony and honeymoon are over, it is surprising how swiftly your wedding anniversary comes around each year. The weeks and months turn into years very quickly, and busy lives can often take a toll on love and romance. Taking the time to allow yourselves to continue and renew the vestiges of your courtship period will keep the marriage fresh, exciting, and healthy. Human relationships are living things and without a little daily attention, and occasional dramatic and bold measures, the marriage can began to feel dull and stagnant. If your marriage starts to slip off course, use your imagination to do something different, fun, and sometimes even spectacular! Pay as much attention to each other as you do to your jobs, hobbies, and cars, and marriage bliss and longevity is more likely to be a reality.

It doesn't take untold time, energy, or extraordinary measures to keep the embers of love aglow as the years pass. Communication is one of the essential keys. Allow yourselves time to communicate, and on occasion, to do this in an uninterrupted atmosphere. Take the time to do the little things that say without words, "I Love You." A surprise weekend away, a small bouquet of flowers, a sweet note in your partner's lunch, mutual help and cooperation regarding the responsibilities of home and family, will breathe continual romance, fun, and love into the union. A little remembrance can turn an ordinary day into something special for each of you. As an old love song goes:

> Blow me a kiss from across the room.
> Say I look nice when I'm not.
> A line a day when you're far away.
> Little things mean a lot.
>
> *Edith Lindeman and Carol Stutz*

Scheduling time together, much the same as when you were dating, is one way to insure that you don't neglect your marriage. Shopping for groceries together at different stores can be fun to do from time to time. Taking in a matinee or museum beforehand can make you look forward to the ordinary event of grocery shopping with renewed interest.

Spend one full evening each week together without the television on, working on a fun-to-do home project. It's impossible to carry on an interesting conversation when the box is squawking at you. It demands your full attention. Shut it off and give your full and undivided attention to each other to plan out a family vacation, review your financial directions, start a special home project, or simply take a long walk together after dinner.

When children arrive on the scene, give them a regular and early bedtime each night, so that you will continue to have time alone together, before you have to get up and start the process of making your daily living and caring for a home and family all over again. Children need their sleep to grow and to learn each day, and you both need and deserve time together each evening to continue the intimacy, romance, fun, and laughter in your marriage.

When the weather permits, rent a canoe and paddle down a lazy river together. A warm, lazy summer day, spent together in the close confines of a small canoe, can be fun and promotes communication. Surprise your spouse with handwritten "love letters in the sand" at the beach. In winter, never pass up a walk together during a driving snowstorm. Write a surprise love note in the snow. Relax in front of the fire together with a good book on a cold and snowy winter evening. Enjoy each other's silence as much as each other's conversation.

Plan one "easy menu night" a week, as far as mealtime goes. A scaled down menu one night a week not only lightens the load of the cook, but can pave the way for better health. Instead of a big meal, share a bowl of soup and sandwich together over a game of scrabble or cards.

Take mini-honeymoons throughout your married life. Sensible distribution of available income and a desire to focus your attention, completely, for a short period of time on each other once again, is all it takes to do this. Take in a bed and breakfast close to home. Go on a weekend bike tour. Find a cozy inn to spend a night that offers a hay ride or a sleigh ride and a warm fireplace for your comfort afterwards.

Tell your friends and families that you are going away and simply stay home and out of sight. Have a "for your eyes only" weekend together. Plan a special meal with special music and special everything to go with it. Exchange houses or apartments with a family member or friend and have your special weekend in a new and different setting. Meaningful, fun-filled time together is an important ingredient for a long and lasting, intimate marriage.

⮞ Renewing Your Marriage Vows

One of the ways to recapture memories of your courtship and your wedding day is to renew you marriage vows every few years. Renewing your vows every five years or so will force you to take a good look at your marriage and know for sure if it is going in the right direction, and if not, what needs to be done to repair it.

Some religious groups offer inexpensive encounters or retreats to help couples accomplish this. These are usually group experiences that review marriage life in general with an exchange of information among couples about where their marriage is at and how they got there—a sort of time out, away from all responsibilities, for honest reflection and communication on the fabric of your marriage, and repair strategies if needed. At the conclusion of the encounter, each couple renews their marriage vows in front of the congregation.

If you would like this to be a private occasion, there are many ways that this can be done. Some couples may make renewing their vows a special family occasion. Others may choose to renew their marriage vows during the privacy of a long-awaited vacation to a very special place such as Paris, "the city of eternal romance." You can take in all the romantic sites and plan to repeat your marriage vows here also.

The Hotel Lancaster, a small, deluxe establishment, 30 seconds from the Champs Elysees in Paris, France, will shower you with attention and make repeating your marriage vows a reality in their luxurious accommodations with an intimate garden courtyard. The hotel was built in 1899 and was originally a family home of Santiago Drake del Castillo. "Many distinguished guests stay here and regard it as their 'pied à terre' (little apartment) in Paris." If you would like to investigate Paris for a place to renew your marriage and your marriage vows, write or call M. Francois Touzin, 7 rue de Berri, Champs Elysee, 75008 Paris, France, 01-1-43-59-90-43.

⮞ Creating a Lasting Marriage

Before your wedding day arrives, ponder the beautiful words of these wise poets. Set your marriage course according to their verses and keep these words locked away in your hearts for a marriage that is true, happy, and everlasting.

Any Wife or Husband

Let us be guests in one another's house
With deferential "No" and courteous "Yes";
Let us take care to hide our foolish moods
Behind a certain show of cheerfulness.

Let us avoid all sullen silences;
We should find fresh and sprightly things to say;
I must be fearful lest you find me dull,
And you must dread to bore me any way.

Let us knock gently at each other's heart,
Glad of a chance to look within—and yet
Let us remember that to force one's way
Is the unpardoned breach of etiquette.

So shall I be hostess—you, the host—
Until all need for entertainment ends;
We shall be lovers when the last door shuts,
But what is better still—we shall be friends.

Carol Haynes

Need of Loving

Folk need a lot of loving in the morning;
The day is all before, with cares beset—
The cares we know, and they that give no warning;
for love is God's own antidote for fret.

Folk need a heap of loving at the noontime—
In the battle lull, the moment snatched from strife—
Halfway between the waking and the croontime,
While bickering and worriment are rife.

Folk hunger so for loving at the nighttime,
When wearily they take them home to rest
At slumber song and turning-out-the-light time
Of all the times for loving, that's the best.

Folk want a lot of loving every minute
The sympathy of others and their smile!
Till life's end, from the moment they begin it,
Folk need a lot of loving all the while.

Strickland Gillilan

If You're Ever Going to Love Me

If you're ever going to love me love me, while I can know
All the sweet and tender feelings which from real affection flow.
Love me now, while I am living; do not wait till I am gone
And then chisel it in marble—warm love words on ice-cold stone.
If you've dear, sweet thoughts about me, why not whisper them to me?
Don't you know 'twould make me happy and as glad as glad could be?
If you wait till I am sleeping, ne'er to waken here again,
There'll be walls of earth between us and I couldn't hear you then.
If you knew someone was thirsting for a drop of water sweet
Would you be so slow to bring it? Would you step with laggard feet?
There are tender hearts all round us who are thirsting for our love;
Why withhold from them what nature makes them crave all else above?
I won't need your kind caresses when the grass grows o'er my face;
I won't crave your love or kisses in my last low resting place.
So, then, if you love me any, if it's but a little bit,
Let me know it now while living; I can own and treasure it.

Unknown

Never forget the ten ingredients of a successful marriage:

1. Patience
2. Kindness
3. Respect
4. Fair play
5. Honesty
6. Fortitude
7. Laughter
8. Order
9. Remembrance
10. Love

⚜ Notable Quotations on Love and Marriage

To keep your marriage brimming with love in the loving cup,
whenever you're wrong, admit it;
whenever you're right, shut up.

Ogden Nash

Kindness is the life's blood, the elixir of marriage. Kindness makes the difference between passion and caring. Kindness is tenderness. Kindness is love, but perhaps greater than love. . . Kindness is good will. Kindness says, I want you to be happy.

Randolph Ray

Marriage is our last best chance to grow up.

Joseph Barth

It took great courage to ask a beautiful young woman to marry me. Believe me, it is easier to play the whole of Petrushka on the piano.

Arthur Rubinstein

Make sure you never argue at night. You just lose a good night's sleep and you can't settle anything until morning anyway.

Rose Kennedy

Love is the only sane and satisfactory answer to the problem of human existence.

Erich Fromm

To keep the fire burning brightly there's one easy rule: Keep the two logs together, near enough to keep each other warm and far enough apart—about a finger's breath—for breathing room. Good fire, good marriage, same rule.

Marnie Reed Cromwell

A successful marriage requires falling in love many times, always with the same person.

Migon McLaughlin

My most brilliant achievement was my ability to be able to persuade my wife to marry me.

Winston Churchill

Where love rules, there is no will to power; and where power predominates, there love is lacking.

Carl Jung

The crime of love is forgetting.

Maurice Chevalier

An archaeologist is the best husband a woman can have. The older she gets, the more interested he is in her.

Agatha Christie

You will reciprocally promise love, loyalty and matrimonial honesty. We only want for you this day that these words constitute the principle of your entire life and that with the help of divine grace, you will observe these solemn vows that today, before God, you formulate.

Pope Paul II

The love we have in our youth is superficial compared to the love an old man has for his old wife.

Will Durant

I would like to have engraved inside every wedding band "Be Kind To Each Other." This is the Golden Rule of marriage and the secret of making love last through the years.

Randolph Ray

The truth [is] that there is only one terminal dignity—love. And the story of a love is not important—what is important is that one is capable of love. It is perhaps the only glimpse we are permitted of eternity.

Helen Hayes

Bibliography

Arisian, Khoren. *The New Wedding: Creating Your Own Marriage Ceremony.* New York: Vintage Books, 1973.

Eichler, Lillian. *The Customs of Mankind.* Garden City, N.Y.: Garden City Publishers, 1924.

Emerson, Ralph Waldo. *The Works of Emerson.* Roslyn, N.Y.: Black's Readers Service Co.

Felleman, Hazel, ed. *The Best Loved Poems of the American People.* New York: Doubleday, 1936.

Gibran, Khalil. *The Prophet.* New York: Alfred A. Knopf, 1972.

Gibran, Khalil. *The Voice of the Master.* The Citadel Press, N.Y., 1958.

Lindbergh, Anne Morrow. *Gifts from the Sea.* New York: Pantheon Books, 1955.

Longfellow, Henry Wadsworth. *Favorite Poems of Henry Wadsworth Longfellow.* Garden City, N.Y.: Doubleday, 1967.

Simpson, James B., comp. *Simpson's Contemporary Quotations: The Most Notable Quotes Since 1950.* Boston: Houghton Mifflin, 1988.

Wallis, Charles L. *Our American Heritage.* New York: Harper and Row, 1970.

Best in Children's Books. Garden City, N.Y.: Nelson Doubleday, Inc. 1959.

Marriage in the Episcopal Church. Fourteenth (Revised) Printing. Cincinnati, Ohio: Forward Movement Publications.

Index

A

accessories, fabric store, 17
Adinkra, 112
African wedding broomsticks, 111
agent, travel, questions for, 148
Alcoholics Anonymous, prayer of, 100
Algoma Central Railway, 155
Alixis Event Coordinators, 8
alterations, 27
  charge for, 30
  of recycled bridal, 66
American Accompaniment Track Tapes, 68
American Association of Retired Persons, 70
Anastasio, Janet and Bevilaqua, Michelle, *The*
  Everything Wedding Book, 74
anniversaries, 196
announcements, designing, 41-50
Apache marriage blessing, 88
apparel
  bridesmaids
    color, 21-22
    custom made, 22
  maid of honor, color, 22
  mothers of the bride and groom, 33-39
  wedding, considerations for, 21-31
artist
  sketch, 10
  sketches of ceremony and reception by, 10
Ashanti, 109
attire
  mother's
    color coordinating with wedding party, 36-37
    guidelines for choosing, 37-39
  mothers', coordinating, 36
  period, historic, 3
  source for bridal, thriftstore, 36
Audiopictures, 59
  sample, 60f

B

Baba, Yoriko, 116
Barr, Diane, 8
Barth, Joseph, 201
Barzak, Rhoda, 9
basic dress styles, 38-39fbaskets
  apple, 15
  flower, 15
Bevilaqua, Michelle. *See* Anastasio, Janet
bird baths, 16
Blue Waters Beach Hotel, 135
bookstore, source for personalizing ceremony, 19
bouquet, bridal, present to friend, 100
Brichcraft Thermographers, 100
Bridal Belles, 137
budget, 63, 66

intimate ceremony, 69
Burlington, Vermont, 136

C

cake, wedding, 19
  ceramic tops, 96
  glassblown topper, 96
  shortcake with strawberries, 92
  theme tops, 95
  various shapes, 95
candy, in favors, 99
Canyoneers, Inc., 131
catalog, rental of bridal attire, 67
centerpieces, fruit as, 18
ceremonies
  Afro-American, 108-112
    attire, 108-109
    bell-ringer, 109
    broom, source for, 111
    colors, 109
      red, 110
    flowers, 112
    instruments, 112
    invitations, 111
    Jumping the Broom, 110
    Libation, 109
    music, 111
    wedding dress, source for, 111
  for the blind, 121-123
    music, processional and recessional, 122
  at distant locations, 127-149
    African safari, 128, 140
    Agawa Canyon Train Tour, 151-155
    Antigua, 134-135
    apparel for, 142-143
    Bermuda, 137-138
    Caribbean, 128
    Cayman Islands, 139-140
    cruises, 131, 130
    Europe, 128
    Fiji, 128, 134
    Grand Canyon, 128, 131-132
    Green Mountain Flyer (train), 155-156
    hot-air balloons, 156-157
    lead time, 128
    license requirements, 129-130
    Middlethorpe Hall, York, England, 141
    New England, 128
    organizer checklist, 144-146
    questions for, 149
    questions for travel agent, 148
    reception/celebration party, 149
    S/V Fantome (Bahamas Wedding), 130
    S/V Flying Cloud (British Virgin Island Wedding),
      130

Salzburg, Austria, 138
San Antonio, 141-142
South Pacific, 128
St. Kitts, West Indies, 132-133
travel advisories, 143-144
travel agent for, 147
U.S. Virgin Islands, 133
Vail, Colorado, 128, 136-137
Vermont, 135-136
for the hearing impaired, 123-124
    music, 124
    signing, 123
Hispanic-American
    arriahs, 113
    bible, 114
    crowns, 114
    finances, 115
    flowers, 113
    La Biborita, 113
    laso, 112
    mantilla, 113
    music, 114-115
    rings, 113
    wedding attire, 114
    wedding consultant, 115
Japanese, 115-116
for physically challenged, 119-125
    attire for, 120
    dancing at reception, 121
    additional ideas, 124-125
various countries and cultures, 116-117
ceremony
    benediction, 87-88
    declaration of marriage, 85
    format for, 73-74
    homily, 82
    introduction of couple, 88
    opening words, 76-78
    poetry, 81-82
    prayers
        childrens, 80
        clergy, 78
        closing, 86-87
        of support, 83
    processional, entrance of bride and groom, 101
    promises from bride and groom, 82-83
    question to couple from clergy, 82
    reading, bride and groom, 85-86
    readings, 79-80
    religious, 73
    rings
        blessing
        exchange of, 85
    ring's symbol, 84-85
    scripture, 78-79
    support of marriage, 83
    unity candle, 83
    vows, 84
Cha Cha, 115
chapels, wedding, 9

Chevalier, Maurice, 202
Child, Julia and Beck, Simone, *Mastering the Art of French Cooking,* 117
children
    doll carriages or cart at ceremony, 10
    as part of parent's wedding ceremony, 7
Children of a Lesser God, 119
Christie, Agatha, 202
Churchill, Winston, 201
circumstances, special
    second marriage, 2
    second marriage and children, 6
    wedding of grandparents, 2
Classic Collectin, 67
clergy, licensed to perform marriage, 88
clip art, 41
clothing repair kit, 179
color
    favorite in choice of gowns, 22
    harmony, 25
    in men's attire, 26
    as patchwork quilt, 26
    swatches at fabric store, 17
    use of as accent, 4
    use of hues, 25
    use of tones, 25
    wheel, 25
colors
    appropriateness of, 24
    for bridesmaids, 23
    combinations, 24-26
    matching with wedding day environment, 23
    seasonal choices, 24
communication, in marriage, 196
consultant, wedding, 8, 115, 116
    Correia, Deborah, 137
    Goddard, Kristen, 137
Cook, Sharon C. and Gale, Elizabeth, *Personal Wedding Planner, A,* 74
Coronet Thermographers, 100
Correia, Deborah, 137-138
costumes, period, 8
cows, 6
Cox, Beverly and Jacobs, Martin, *Spirit of the Harvest North American Indian Cooking, The,* 117
creativity, sources, 14
    crafts store, 17-18
    fabric shop, 17
    garden shop, 14-16
Cromwell, Marnie Reed, 201
customs
    Greek, 167
    wedding, 167-170
Cutler
    Jullian S., *Through the Year,* 82-83
    Rabbi Jerome. *See* Hall, Marilyn

D
date, wedding, seasonal, 68
decorating, seasonal, 68

Departure Checklist, 146f
diary, wedding day, 10
disc jockeys, 69
　and loud music, 94
Distant Wedding Organizer, 145f
Doke, Mimi, 115
doll carriage, 10
doves, 100
dress, mother's
　borrowing, 35
　color, 34
　delivery date, 34
　questions in choosing, 33-34
　ready-made, 34
　reusing, 35-36
　sizes, 34
　source for, 35-36
　style, 33
　thrift shop, 36
Durant, Will, 202
Dzynes, Rose, 8

E
Edwards, Rev. Dale R., 82
Eklof, Barbara, "With These Words. . . I Thee Wed:"
　Contemporary Wedding Vows for Today's Couple, 74
Emerson, Ralph Waldo, 79
envelopes
　with colored liner, 42
　double or single, 42
　from wedding invitation companies, 42
Ethnicity, Inc, 111

F
fabrics
　for bridesmaids, 22-23
　variety for gowns, 22
Fantasy Balloon Flights, 156-157
favors
　bookmarks, 99
　boxes, 100
　candy, 19
　candy and nuts in netting, 99
　cloth roses, 97
　at crafts store, 18
　fruit as, 18
　potpourri, 99
　seedlings, 4
　thumb print pictures, 10-11
Fell, Derek, Encyclopedia of Flowers, 117
Fitzgibbon, Theodora, Taste of Ireland, A, 117
flowers
　at crafts store, 17
　on doll carriage, 10
　Gardenias, 98
　hanging, 14
　Jasmine, 99
　Lavande Rose, 98
　Lavender, 99
　McGredy Ivory Rose, 98
　meanings of, 172
　Mother Orchid, 98
　Plumeria, 98
　potted, 15
　Royalty Red Rose, 98
　silk, 17
　Stephanotis, 98, 122
　Sweet William, 98
　Victory Rose, 98
Fromm, Erich, 201

G
Gale, Elizabeth. See Cook, Sharon C.
Ghana, West Africa, 108-109
Gibran
　Kahlil, 46
　Khalil, from The Prophet, 81
gifts, special, quilt, 3
Gillian, Strickland, 199
glassblowers, 96
Goddard, Kristen, 137
Golden Lemon, 132
gowns
　bridal
　　alterations, 27
　　alterations availabilty, 29-30
　　alterations charge, 30
　　borrowing, 67
　　colors, 28
　　embellishing, 64
　　fabrics, 28
　　laces, 29
　　need for in-house seamstress, 30
　　order time-frame, 29
　　quality assurance of manufacturer, 29
　　questions when purchasing, 28-31
　　recycling mother's wedding dress, 66
　　renting, 67
　　"restocking" charge, 30
　　self-decorated, 26
　　self-made, 26
　　shipping date, 29
　　size change after ordering, 30
　　size charts, 28
　bridemaids, reusing, 22
　bridesmaids
　　cotton print, 24
　　wearability, 22
　custom made, skirt length, 22
　for expectant brides, 27-28
Green Mountain Flyer, 156
greenware, 96

H
Hall, Marilyn and Cutler, Rabbi Jerome, Celebrity
　Kosher Cookbook, The, 117
Hayes, Helen, 202
Haynes, Carol, 199
hayride, 7

Hazelton, Nika Standen, *Best Italian Cooking, The,* 117
herbs, 16
  strewing on family members, 100
Hershey Company, 99
Hilton Chefs, *Hilton International Cookbook,* 117
honeymoons, 195-196
Horiuchi, Shin, 116
horses, 5, 7-8
Hortense Hewett, 99

I
Inn at Essex, 136
instruments, musical, Shaum (oboe), 8
insurance, and photography, 52
International Ventures, 140
interpreters, and sign language, 123
invitation, preserving, 49-50
  in a mirror, 50
  in pewter, 50
  on Vermont marble, 49
invitations
  clip art, 41
  design of, 8
  designing, 41-50
  envelope size, 41
  original ideas, 43-44
  paper stock for, 42
  sample, 44f
  sample B, 45f
  use of printer as consultant, 42

J
Jacobs, Martin. *See* Cox, Beverly
Jandi Rentals, 67
Jessica McClintock, 34
Jones, Tammey D., 111
Jung, Carl, 202

K
Kennedy, Rose, 201
Kente cloth, 108-109
knobs, wooden, as chess set, 18
Kotobuki, 115

L
La Mansion del Rio, 141-142
Lake Champlain, 136
Libation, 109
Library of Nations, 117
Lindberg, Anne Morrow, 79
love, rekindling, 196-197
Lovejoy, John, 59

M
Mambo, 115
Mariachi, 114
market, fruit, 18
marriage
  creating a lasting, 198-200

quotations on, 200-203
  successful, ingredients for, 200
marriage vows, renewing, 198
Matlin, Marlee, 119
McLaughlin, Migon, 201
memory making, 159-173
Middlethorpe Hall, York, England, 141
Monchstein Castle, Salzburg, Austria, 138
motorcycles, as used in weddings, 9
Mt. Kenya Cathedral, 140
music, 19
  hymns, 75
  preludes, 74
  processionals, 75
  recessionals, 75
  sing-along, 68
  vocal, 75
musicians, woodwinds, 5

N
Nash, Ogden, 200
National Public Radio, 75
National Wildlife Federation, 173
Newport Beach, California, 9
newsrelease
  dress descriptions, 184
  fabric names for, 183-184
  gown details and embellishments descriptions for, 189-190
  guidelines for, 183-193
  headpiece descriptions for, 192
  hemline descriptions, 189
  lace descriptions for, 191
  neckline descriptions, 185
  outline for, 192-193
  skirt and waistline descriptions, 186-187
  sleeve descriptions, 188
  trains descriptions for, 189
  veil description for, 191
  veiling types descriptions for, 191
Nigeria, 108
notebook, for creative ideas, 13-14
Noye, Rev. Worth, 82

O
Oceanside, California, 8
ordering, tuxedos, 31
Ormond Beach, Florida, 9

P
Palmer, Albert, 107
paper
  from arts supply store, 42
  from catalog, 42
parents, divorced, 3
Patty, Heidi, 140
Peterson, Rev. Courtney, 77, 84, 85
Phillips, Marcia, 59
photographer, use of professional, 51-61
photography

film, 52
 keys to good, 51-53
 multiple pose technique, 52
 questions for, 52
 strobe lights, 52
 viewing work of your photographer, 52
pictures
 candids, 56-57
 creative
  black and white, 56
  bridal bouquet, 54
  double exposures, 55
  empty wedding shoes, 55
  families within families, 55
  reflective, 54
  sepia-toned, 56
  sequencing, 56
  silhouette, 54
  star filter, 56
  vignetting, 54
  weather, 54
 shooting prior to ceremony, 56
 using family home, 55
 wedding
  illustrative, 53
  posing, 53
   fashion, 53
   traditional, 53
poles, hanging, 14
Pope Paul II, 202
printer, as consultant for invitations, 42
program
 information for, 48
 sample, 48f
programs, 45
 design for, 47
 quotations for, 46
publisher, desktop, 41
publishing, desktop, designing announcements and
 invitations, 41

R
Ray, Randolph, 201, 202
receipts, bridal log book, 70-71
reception
 dancing, 94
 head table, 92-93
 music
  disc jockeys, 94
  loud, 94
 seating of guests, 93
 sing-a-longs, 94
 special diet foods, 96
 swimming, 91
 tables, round, 93
 tent party, 91
 white-water rafting, 92
recycling, bridal attire, 65
relatives, uncooperative, 178-179
rings, 113

wedding, for children of bride and groom, 7
roses, cloth
 for bird seed, 97
 instructions for, 97
Rubinstein, Arthur, 201

S
Sakaki tree, 115
sales, 63
Salsa, 115
Sanko, Margaret, 140
scrolls, 45
seams, finishing of, 27
seamstress, 64
 alterations by, 27
 as professional, 30
 competence of, 27
 designing mother's gown, 37
 to make bridesmaids gowns, 22
seed, bird, 97
sewing, 64
 personal wedding gown, 26
shoes
 dyeing, 30-31
 rental with tuxedo, 31
shop
 bake, 18-19
 bridal, in-house seamstress, 30
 garden
  baskets, 15
  bird baths, 16
  bulbs, 15
  hanging poles and plants, 1415
  herbs, 15
  Japanese stepping stones, 16
  trees, flowering, 16
signing, 123
Simone, Beck. See Child, Julia
sites, memorable, 4
 barn with cows, 6
 camping, 5-6
 hot air balloon, 11
 shipboard, 11
 ski lodge, 4
Spanish Bay Reef, 139
stones, Japanese stepping, 16
store
 candy, 19
 crafts
  favors, 18
  silk flowers, 17
 hardware, 18
 music, 19
strobe lights, 52

T
toast, use of various languages, 3
toasts, 103-106
 with water, 101
T. R. Thornton Wedding Apparel Company, 64

traditions, ethnic, 107-108
transportation
  of bride and groom, horseback, 5
  of guests, hayride, 7
travel advisories, 143-144
trees, flowering, 16
Turtle Holidays, 134
Tux Town, 67
tuxedo, 26
  accessories with rental, 31
  ordering, 31
  rental, 31
Twain, Mark, 80, 86

V
Vail Athletic Club, 136-137
vegetarians, 96
Vermont Stoneworks, 49-50, 61
video, montage, 58
videos, use of professionals, 57-58
visualize, 13-14

W
Wallen, Rev. Drew, 133
Watabe Wedding Services Ltd., 116
wedding, small, 69
wedding disasters
  alternate plan for outside ceremony, 180-181
  alternate wedding apparel, 181
  auxiliary plan for, 179-180
  emergency kit for, 179
  flowers, 181
  turning into celebrations, 175-182
Wedding Fantasies, 137-138
weddings, theme
  camping, 5
  Caribbean, 4
  farm, 6-7
  historical, 8
  "Leather and Lace," 9
  old fashioned country style, 7-8
  Renaissance, 8
  Revolutionary War, 3
  skiing, 4
wheelchairs, 120
  decorating, 125
White Rose Weddings, 9
Wilson, Donna, 9
Winans, B. B. and C. C., *I.O.U. Me*, 110
Windjammer Barefoot Cruises, 130
wishing pretzels, 167